ADMIRING GOD

ADMIRING GOD

The best of George Müller

Edited by

Roger Steer

HODDER AND STOUGHTON
LONDON SYDNEY AUCKLAND TORONTO

British Library C.I.P. Data

Müller, George, *1805–1898*
  Admiring God : The best of George Müller.
  1. Christian life
  I. Title   II. Steer, Roger
  248.4   BV4501.2

ISBN 0 340 39941 4

Hodder and Stoughton Editorial Office: 47 Bedford Square, London WC1B 3DP.

CONTENTS

INTRODUCTION

George Müller believed . . .

. . . that God answers prayer, and devoted his life to demonstrating the truth of this assertion. His efforts brought him fame even during his lifetime, and a letter from a doctor telling him his achievement was 'the most wonderful and complete refutation of scepticism' he had ever come across was typical of many he received. I suspect that he would have regarded the verdict of an early biographer – W. H. Harding (1914) – that the story of his (Müller's) life presented 'one of the most striking testimonies to the faithfulness of God that the world has ever seen' as an exaggeration, although I think he would have conceded that at least this assessment accorded the honour where it was rightfully due.

Müller died in his ninety-third year, and his writings and recorded sermons amount to well over one million words. As far as I am aware, this is the first book to bring together the best of his writings and addresses on a wide range of subjects. I think that Müller is worth listening to for three reasons.

First, there was the *intensity of his relationship with God*. At his graveside, Mr G. F. Bergin said that Müller 'communed with God in prayer, perhaps more than any other man of the century, perhaps more than any other man who ever lived; his communion with God was his native breath, he lived in an attitude of prayer'. He himself said, 'No-one ever knew Jehovah without being able to exercise faith in Him. It is when God is not known that difficulty comes.'

Second, there was his *unparalleled love of the Bible*. A. N. Wilson has recently observed that 'in every generation, there have been people who have seen the simple force of what Thomas à Kempis saw: "If you would understand Christ's words fully and taste them truly, you must strive to form your whole life after His pattern."' Müller was such a man in his generation.

His theological training at the University of Halle, his association with the talented young men who are now seen as the founders of the Brethren movement (though they would have been horrified to have been seen as the founders of a movement), his passion for the Hebrew language and the personal commitment of his whole life to God in the summer of 1829 were the prelude to a lifetime's delight in the Bible. It was his rule in his personal life; it was his guide in directing the affairs of Bethesda chapel, the church in Bristol of which he was pastor for over sixty years.

In a letter he wrote to the (then) British and Foreign Bible Society towards the end of his life, he referred in passing to the fact that he had read the whole Bible through 'considerably more than one hundred times with prayer and meditation'. His son-in-law revealed, 'I hardly ever went into his room but the Bible was open. When no break in his ordinary life occurred, seven, eight or ten chapters were his ordinary reading. He fed on the Bread of Life and that was why he was strong when other men were weak.'

The third reason why Müller deserves our attention is what we may call the *Müller phenomenon*. By this, I refer to the successful venture of faith he embarked upon just as Charles Dickens, in *Oliver Twist*, was drawing the British public's attention to the plight of orphans. 'Now if I,' he decided, 'a poor man, simply by prayer and faith, obtained, without asking any individual, the means for establishing and carrying on an orphan house; there would be something which, with the Lord's blessing, might be instrumental in strengthening the faith of the children of

8

God, besides being a testimony to the consciences of the unconverted of the reality of the things of God.'

Following a public meeting in Bristol in 1835 when he announced his intention (but at which of course there was deliberately no collection), gifts in money and in kind began to be sent to Müller's home: furniture, cutlery, clothing and materials. A woman who earned less than ten shillings a week from needlework gave Müller one hundred pounds. A husband and wife told him they would like to work in his orphanage if he thought them well enough qualified.

And so it went on. One hundred and fifty years ago this year (in April 1836), Müller was able to open his first children's home in a rented house in Wilson Street, Bristol, for thirty girls aged between 7 and 12.

Though he went quietly about his work, this little home amounted to a challenge to unbelievers to watch the work Müller had begun, to see if there was a God who would finance it. And here was a challenge to Christians not only to see what God would do, but to consider their response if He proved faithful.

There are not many sagas in the history of the Christian Church which can equal the excitement and drama of the next sixty-two years. Müller received nearly one and a half million pounds and the various branches of his work included the care of some ten thousand children, at first in four rented homes and then in five enormous houses purpose built by Müller on Ashley Down, on the outskirts of Bristol. These buildings are now the headquarters of Brunel Technical College (though the work he founded still flourishes in Bristol, Clevedon and Weston-super-Mare).

In addition to the residential care of children, Müller sent thousands of pounds abroad to support hundreds of missionaries all over the world. He established schools in Spain, India, Italy, British Guiana and in many counties of England and Wales. Through the Scriptural Knowledge Institution, which he directed and which also still exists, he circulated Bibles, books and tracts in many countries.

All the money to finance these activities was raised without any advertising, jumble sales, sponsored walks, fundraising committees or appeals for funds of any kind.

In the early years there were trying periods when Müller had no reserves of funds, and his journal for this period is full of cliff-hanging accounts of how money arrived at his children's homes only hours or even minutes before it was needed. Some of these delightfully told stories are included among the readings which make up this book. Müller insisted that no child ever went without nourishing food or a needed item of clothing – an assertion which is borne out by the respect in which he was always held in Bristol.

Finally, what sort of man was Müller? He rarely allowed himself to be photographed, but I suspect that a well-known portrait he did allow is misleading. Certainly it indicates a man of integrity and powerful personality, but I am sure it exaggerates the element of sternness. This may simply reflect the Victorian custom of never smiling in a photograph – partly the result of having to stand quite still for several seconds while the slow time exposure recorded its image on film!

Arthur Pierson, who knew him well, referred to the

smile which so habitually lit up his eyes and played over his features that it left its impress on the lines of his face . . . he relished a joke that was free of all taint of uncleanness and that had about it no sting for others. To those whom he best knew and loved he showed his true self, in his playful moods – as when at Ilfracombe – climbing with his wife and others the heights that overlook the sea, he walked on a little in advance, seated himself till the rest came up with him and then, when they were barely seated, rose and quietly said, 'Well now, we have had a good rest, let us go on.'

Charles Parsons recalled the surprise he had at his first ever sight of Müller (then an old man) with 'his devoted wife strolling about in front of No. 3 Orphan House, stopping leisurely now and again, admiring the flowers that adorned the grounds'.

One of the themes which will emerge again and again in the readings which follow is the theme of happiness. He told a group of young men in 1873:

> It would pain me to the utmost if people could live with me a month in the house and not bear this testimony – that Mr Müller is 'a happy man' . . . There is something unspeakably blessed in this, that the older one gets, the nearer the end of the journey, the brighter the blessedness of the prospect; with Heaven as one's home, that one is getting nearer and nearer to the gates.

Certainly, he was heavenly minded – and we may recall the words of C. S. Lewis: 'Evangelicals who abolished the Slave Trade, all left their mark on earth, precisely because their minds were occupied with Heaven. It is since Christians have largely ceased to think of the other world that they have become so ineffective in this.' And Müller was certainly of earthly use – even judged by the standards of earthly men and women. Indeed he was in some respects a pioneer in the care of children. Admittance to other orphanages was at that time normally gained, not according to the relative needs of the child, but upon personal recommendation or by a majority of votes at periodic meetings of subscribers. In Müller's case, subscribers' meetings were not held, and his example gradually led to the abolition of the voting system altogether.

His character shines through his writings. Rarely (this is particularly true of his middle and later years) does he attack anything. He was *for* God, *for* happiness, *for* goodness, *for* that which is wholesome. There is nothing negative, never a hint of cynicism. He chose his words carefully and wrote with precision. Though a trained theologian, he was not much interested in abstract doctrine. He liked to apply Biblical truths to everyday living,

11

and saw it his business to express profound truths in simple, understandable terms.

I have made some editorial changes to the text, mainly where necessary by reducing the length of Müller's sentences and occasionally updating an archaic word or phrase. The only other change I have made is to reproduce verses of Scripture in the New International Version, rather than the Authorised Version generally used by Müller.

On pages 13–14 I have listed the main events of Müller's life. Also, I have arranged the readings chronologically so that you can, in a sense, live through the main events and concerns of his life. You will see something of the growth of the man and his ideas. On some subjects, there is less certainty and more diffidence towards the end. But on his main theme, the conviction grew stronger – that God was and is the living God. And the secret of life is to delight yourself in Him.

Roger Steer

MAIN EVENTS OF MÜLLER'S LIFE

1805 (September 27)	Born, Kroppenstaedt, Prussia
1810	The family move to Heimersleben. His father is appointed collector of taxes
1820	His mother dies
1821	Arrested for debt in Wolfenbüttel. Spends four weeks in prison
1825 (Easter)	Enters Halle University to study theology under Friedrich Tholuck
1825 (November)	Becomes a Christian following a visit to a small house meeting
1828 (March)	Graduates at Halle
1829 (January)	Rejected from army service on grounds of 'a tendency to tuberculosis'
1829 (March)	Arrives in London to train with the London Society for Promoting Christianity among the Jews (now the Church Mission to the Jews)
1829 (May)	Falls ill. Believes he is dying
1829 (Summer)	Convalescence in Teignmouth, Devon. Meets Henry Craik and becomes associated with the founders of Brethren movement.
1830 (January)	Ends association with London Society for Promoting Christianity among the Jews
1830	Becomes pastor of Ebenezer chapel in Teignmouth
1830 (August)	Marries Mary Groves (sister of Anthony Norris Groves) in Exeter
1830 (October)	Pew-rents abandoned at Ebenezer chapel. Müller gives up a regular salary
1832 (May)	Müller and Henry Craik accept an invitation to become pastors of Gideon chapel in Bristol
1832 (June)	Müller and Craik begin to work at Bethesda chapel, Bristol
1832 (September)	Lydia Müller (their only child to survive infancy) is born
1834	Establishes Scriptural Knowledge Institution for Home and Abroad

13

1836 (April)	Opens first children's home in Wilson Street, Bristol, for thirty children. Subsequently opens three further homes in same street
1837 (June)	Princess Victoria becomes Queen
1841	His father dies
1848	Split between 'Open' and 'Exclusive' Brethren (followers of J. N. Darby)
1849 (June)	Opens new purpose-built home on Ashley Down, Bristol, for three hundred children (now Allen House)
1857	Second Ashley Down home open (Brunel House)
1862	Third Ashley Down home open (subsequently named Müller House)
1866 (January)	Henry Craik dies
1866	Dr Barnardo opens children's home in London
1869	Fourth Ashley Down home open (Davy House)
1870	Final Ashley Down home open (Cabot House). Müller now cares for two thousand children and employs over two hundred staff
1870 (February)	Mary Müller dies
1870s	Sends £10,000 abroad annually to nearly two hundred missionaries
1871 (November)	Marries Susannah Sangar
1875	Begins preaching tours. Travels two hundred thousand miles to forty-two countries
1878 (January)	Meets President of the United States and (with Susannah) is conducted round the White House
1881	Church of England's Children's Society opens first home
1890 (January)	Lydia Wright (his daughter) dies
1892 (May)	Last preaching tour ends
1894 (January)	Susannah Müller dies
1895 (September)	Ninetieth birthday presentation at Bethesda chapel
1897 (June)	Preaches at Bethesda chapel on occasion of Queen Victoria's Diamond Jubilee
1898 (March 9)	Leads evening prayer meeting on Ashley Down
1898 (March 10)	Dies peacefully at 6.00 a.m., aged 92

Current address of Müller's Homes:
The Müller Homes for Children
Müller House
7 Cotham Park
Bristol BS6 6DA

THEME GUIDE

15

17

SOURCES

Key to abbreviations used at the end of each reading
(JM = Jehovah Magnified)

A *Autobiography of George Müller*, Nisbet, 1914 (third edition)

B Account of a Second Preaching Tour, reproduced in *Jehovah Magnified – Collection of Addresses by George Müller* (JM), Nisbet, 1876

C 'Address to Young Men', delivered in Bethesda chapel, Bristol, 1873 (JM)

D 'Clothed with humility', address at a Monday evening prayer meeting at Salem chapel, Bristol, undated (JM)

E 'The First and Second Adam', address at the Conference of Christians, Clifton, 1866 (JM)

F 'The Forgiving God', sermon preached at the Tabernacle, Penn Street, Bristol, 1876 (JM)

G 'How to Ascertain the will of God', 1895, ECL leaflet

H 'How to become a Successful Labourer in Christ's Vineyard', address at Salem chapel, 1870 (JM)

I 'How to Promote the Glory of God', address at a United Meeting for Prayer, the Broadmead Rooms, Bristol, 1870 (JM)

J Müller's Journal, reproduced in his Narratives (see below)

K 'Love One Another', notes of two addresses delivered at a Conference of Christians at Clifton, October, 1863 (JM)

L 'The Mighty God', address at the Annual Conference of Christians, Clifton, 1870 (JM)

N1 *A Narrative of some of the Lord's Dealings with George Müller*, written by himself, Nisbet, Volume 1, 1869

N2 Volume 2, 1873

N3 Volume 3, 1874

N4 Volume 4, 1886

P 'Parable of the Ten Virgins', notes of a sermon delivered at Bethesda chapel, 1874 (JM)

Q 'The Prayer-Hearing God', a sermon preached in 1880, Bristol Bible and Tract Depot leaflet

R 'The Twenty-Third Psalm', a sermon preached at Bethesda chapel on Jubilee Sunday, 1897, Bristol Bible and Tract Depot leaflet

S 'Satisfied with God', address delivered following the death of his first wife, 1870 (JM)

T 'The Second Coming of Christ', 1881, Bristol Bible and Tract Depot leaflet

U 'The Secret of Effectual Service to God', New Year's address, 1864 (JM)

V 'Unfailing Trust. An Hour's Interview with George Müller' by Charles R. Parsons, 1897, Bristol Bible and Tract Depot leaflet

W 'Unfailing Triumph! Memories of George Müller with many of his choice sayings' by Charles R. Parsons, undated, Bristol Bible and Tract Depot leaflet

X 'Waiting for Christ', address at the Annual Conference of Christians, Clifton, 1870 (JM)

Y 'Walking by Faith, not by Sight', notes of an address at one of the Clifton Conferences of Christians, undated (JM)

READINGS

Constrained by the love of Jesus

Müller became a Christian, while a student at the University of Halle, in November 1825 –

It had pleased God to teach me something of the meaning of that precious truth: 'God so loved the world that he gave his one and only Son, that whoever believes in him shall not perish but have eternal life' (John 3:16). I understood something of the reason why the Lord Jesus died on the cross, and suffered such agonies in the Garden of Gethsemane – that bearing the punishment due to us, we might not have to bear it ourselves. And realising in some measure the love of Jesus for my soul, I was constrained to love Him in return. What all the exhortations and precepts of my father and others could not effect; what all my own resolutions could not bring about, even to renounce a life of sin and profligacy: I was enabled to do, constrained by the love of Jesus.

If you want to have your sins forgiven, you must seek it through the blood of Jesus. If you want power over sin, you must also seek it through the blood of Jesus (N1, 1825).

I remember well the very first evening after my conversion lying peacefully on my bed, knowing that my sins were forgiven, that Heaven was my home, that I was now regenerated, brought on the road to Heaven, and my heart was ready to leap for joy. And ever since matters have gone on in the same way, and this is the blessedness I desire for everyone who is yet without it (R, from a sermon preached at Bethesda chapel on Jubilee Sunday, 1897).

The work of the Spirit

I had now, by the grace of God, some desire to benefit others, and he who so faithfully had once served Satan, sought now to win souls for Christ.

I circulated every month, in different parts of the country [Prussia], about 300 missionary papers. I sold and distributed a considerable number of tracts, and often took my pockets full in my walks, and distributed them, and spoke to poor people whom I met. I wrote letters to some of my former companions in sin.

I visited for thirteen weeks a sick man, who, when I first began to speak to him about the things of God, was completely ignorant of his state as a sinner, trusting for salvation in his upright and moral life. After some weeks, however, the Lord allowed me to see a decided change in him, and he afterwards repeatedly expressed his thanks that I had been sent to him by God to be the means of opening his blind eyes.

Thus the Lord condescended to begin to use me soon after my conversion, though but little; for I did not see at that time, as I do now, that God alone can give spiritual life at first, and keep it up in the soul afterwards.

Once I met a beggar in the fields, and spoke to him about his soul. But when I perceived it made no impression on him, I spoke more loudly; and when he still remained unmoved, I quite bawled in talking to him; till at last I went away seeing it was no use. So ignorant was I of the work of the Spirit, that I thought my speaking very loudly would force into him repentance towards God, and faith in the Lord Jesus (N1, 1826).

First sermon

A schoolmaster asked me whether I would preach in his parish, as the aged and infirm clergyman would be very glad of my assistance. Up to this time I had never preached, though for fifteen months past I might have done so as a student of divinity; for before Christmas 1825 I had been mercifully kept from attempting to preach (though I wrote to my father about July that I had preached, because I knew it would please him), and after Christmas when I knew the Lord, I refrained from doing so, because I felt that I was yet too little instructed in the things of God.

The same reason ought to have still kept me from preaching; yet I thought that by taking a sermon, or the greater part of one, written by a spiritual man, and committing it to memory, I might benefit the people. Had I reasoned scripturally, I should have said surely it cannot be the will of God that I should preach in this way if I have not enough knowledge of the Scriptures to write a sermon. Moreover I had not enough light nor tenderness of conscience to see that I was a deceiver in the pulpit; for everybody supposes that the sermon a man preaches is, if not entirely, at least for the most part his own composition.

I now set about putting a printed sermon into a suitable form, and committing it to memory. It was hard work. It took me nearly a whole week to commit to memory such a sermon as would take up nearly an hour in repeating. I got through it but had no enjoyment in the work. It was on August 27, 1826, at eight in the morning, in a chapel of ease, in connection with which my friend was a school-master (N1, 1826).

Listened to with great attention

At eleven I repeated the same sermon verbatim in the parish church. There was one service more in the afternoon at which I need not have done anything; for the school-master might have read a printed sermon, as he used to do. But having a desire to serve the Lord; and knowing that this aged and unenlightened clergyman had had this living for forty-eight years, and having therefore reason to believe that the Gospel scarcely ever had been preached in that place; I had it in my heart to preach again in the afternoon. But I had no second sermon committed to memory.

It came however to my mind to read Matthew 5, and to make such remarks as I was able. I did so. Immediately upon beginning to expound 'Blessed are the poor in spirit' I felt myself greatly assisted; and whereas in the morning my sermon had not been simple enough for the people to understand it, I was now listened to with the greatest attention, and I think I was also understood. My own peace and joy were great. I felt this a blessed work. After the service I left the aged clergyman as soon as possible lest I should lose my enjoyment . . .

I did not at this time understand the powerlessness of human eloquence. Further I did not keep in mind that if the most illiterate persons in the congregation can comprehend the discourse, the most educated will understand it too; but that the reverse does not hold true (N1, 1826).

The most precious treasure in this life

In January 1827, Müller received a letter from a woman in Frankfurt who signed herself 'An adoring worshipper of the Saviour, Jesus Christ'. He kept the letter, and translated it from the German –

Hold fast the faith which God has given you by His Holy Spirit; it is the most precious treasure in this life, and it contains in itself true happiness. Only seek by watching and prayer more and more to be delivered from all vanity and self-complacency, by which even the true believer may be ensnared when he least expects it. Let it be your chief aim to be more and more humble, faithful, and *quiet*.

May we not belong to those who say and write continually, 'Lord, Lord,' but who have Him not deeply in their hearts. Christianity consists not in words but in power. There must be life in us. For God loved us first that we might love Him in return; and that loving we might receive power to be faithful to Him, and to conquer ourselves, the world, distress, and death. May His Spirit strengthen you for this, that you may be an able messenger of His gospel! (N1, 1827).

God the author

I fell into the snare into which so many young believers fall – the reading of religious books in preference to the Scriptures. I could no longer read French and German novels as I had formerly done to feed my carnal mind; but still I did not put in the place of those books the best of all books. I read tracts, missionary papers, sermons, and biographies of godly persons. The last kind of books I found more profitable than the others, and had they been well selected, or had I not read too much of them, or had any of them served to endear the Scriptures to me, they might have done me much good. I had never been in the habit of reading the Holy Scriptures.

Now the scriptural way of reasoning would have been: God Himself has condescended to become an author, and I am ignorant about that precious Book, which His Holy Spirit has caused to be written through His servants, and it contains that which I ought to know to lead me to true happiness; therefore I ought to read this precious Book most earnestly, most prayerfully, and with much meditation; and in this I ought to continue all the days of my life . . .

But instead of acting thus, for the first four years of my divine life, I preferred the works of uninspired men to the oracles of the living God. In consequence I remained a baby, both in knowledge and in grace (N1, 1827).

The source of all true knowledge

All true knowledge must be derived by the Spirit from the Word. And as I neglected the Word, I was for nearly four years so ignorant that I did not clearly know even the fundamental points of our holy faith. And this lack of knowledge most sadly kept me back from walking steadily in the ways of God. For it is the truth that makes us free (John 8:32) by delivering us from the slavery of the lusts of the flesh, the lusts of the eyes, and the pride of life. The Word proves it. The experience of the saints proves it; and also my own experience most decidedly proves it.

For when it pleased the Lord in August 1829 to bring me really to the Scriptures, my life and walk became very different. And though even since that I have very much fallen short of what I might and ought to be, yet, by the grace of God, I have been enabled to live much nearer to Him than before . . .

If you understand very little of the Word of God, you ought to read it very much; for the Spirit explains the Word by the Word. And if you enjoy reading the Word little, that is just the reason why you should read it much; for the frequent reading of the Scriptures creates a delight in them, so that the more we read them, the more we desire to do so. And if you should be an unbeliever, I would also beg you to read the Scriptures earnestly, and to ask God previously to give you a blessing. For in doing so, God may make you wise for salvation (2 Tim. 3:15), (N1, 1827/1837).

Storing the head with many notions

When we read the Scriptures, it is of the greatest importance to meditate on what we read. Then perhaps a small portion of that which we have read, or if we have time, the whole may be meditated upon in the course of the day. Or a small portion of a book, or an epistle, or a gospel, through which we go regularly for meditation, may be considered every day – without however allowing oneself to be brought into bondage by this plan.

Learned *commentaries* I have found to store the *head* with many notions, and often also with the truth of God; but when the *Spirit* teaches, through the instrumentality of prayer and meditation, the *heart* is affected. The former kind of knowledge generally puffs up, and is often renounced when another commentary gives a different opinion, and often also is found to be good for nothing when it is put into practice. The latter kind of knowledge generally humbles, gives joy, leads us nearer to God, and is not easily reasoned away; and having been obtained from God, and thus having entered into the heart and become our own, is also generally carried out.

If you do not understand the Hebrew and Greek languages, and cannot therefore compare the common translation with the original, you may, concerning several passages, get light by an improved rendering, provided you can be sure that the translator was a truly spiritual person (N1, 1827).

On the road to Berlin

Two ladies of title travelled with me to Berlin in a hired carriage. As I knew that we should be for two days together, I thought in my fleshly wisdom that, though I ought to speak to them about the things of God, I should first show them kindness and attention, and that, after having thus opened a way to their hearts, I might fully set before them their state by nature, and point them to the Lamb of God.

We went on together most amicably, I making only a few

general remarks about divine things. On the second evening however, when we were near the end of our journey, I felt that it was high time to speak. And no sooner had I begun plainly to do so, than one of them replied, 'Oh! Sir, I wish you had spoken sooner about these things, for we have for a long time wished to have someone to whom we might open our hearts; but seeing that the ministers whom we know do not live consistently, we have been kept from speaking to them.'

I now found that they had been under conviction of sin for some time, but did not know the way to obtain peace, even by faith in the Lord Jesus. After this I spoke freely to them during the hour that remained. They parted from me under feelings of gratitude and regret that they could hear no more, for they only passed through Berlin. I felt myself greatly reproved, and all I could do was, by a long letter, to seek to make up for my deficiency in ministering to them on the journey. May this circumstance never be forgotten by me, and may it prove a blessing to the believing reader (N1, 1828).

Kept from spiritual deadness

In March 1829, Müller (then aged 23) arrived in London to train with the London Society for Promoting Christianity among the Jews (now the Church Mission to the Jews) –

I remember what joy it gave me, when a few weeks after my arrival, for the first time, I spoke in English to a little boy, whom I met alone in the fields, about his soul, thinking that he would bear with my broken English.

I now studied much, about twelve hours a day, chiefly Hebrew; commenced Chaldee; perfected myself in reading the German-Jewish in Rabbinic characters, and committed portions of the Hebrew Old Testament to memory. I did this with prayer, often falling on my knees, leaving my books for a little, that I might seek the Lord's blessing, and also that I might be kept from that spiritual deadness which is the result of much study.

I looked up to the Lord even whilst turning over the pages of my Hebrew dictionary, asking His help that I might quickly find the words (N1, 1829).

Our only standard of judgment

A few days after my arrival in Teignmouth, Devon, the chapel called Ebenezer, was re-opened, and I attended the opening. I was much impressed by one of those who preached on the occasion. For though I did not like all he said, yet I saw a gravity and solemnity in him different from the rest. After he had preached, I had a great desire to know more of him; and being invited by two brethren of Exmouth, in whose house he was staying, to spend some time with them, I had an opportunity of living ten days with him under the same roof. Through this brother the Lord bestowed a great blessing upon me, for which I shall have cause to thank Him throughout eternity.

One of the points which God then began to show me was that the Word of God alone is our standard of judgment in spiritual things; that it can be explained only by the Holy Spirit; and that in our day, as well as in former times, He is the teacher of His people. The office of the Holy Spirit I had not experimentally understood before that time. Indeed of the office of each of the blessed persons, in what is commonly called the Trinity, I had no experimental knowledge (N1, 1829).

It is not clear who 'this brother' was. It is unlikely to have been Henry Craik with whom Müller later worked for nearly

31

forty years, but it was obviously one of the influential early figures in the Brethren movement – and it may have been Captain Percy Hall who was at that time preaching in the south Devon area. The next three readings all reflect his influence on Müller.

Principles which stood the test

I had not before seen from the Scriptures that the Father chose us before the foundation of the world; that in Him that wonderful plan of our redemption originated, and that He also appointed all the means by which it was to be brought about.

Further, that the Son, to save us, had fulfilled the law to satisfy its demands, and with it also the holiness of God. And further, that the Holy Spirit alone can teach us about our state by nature, show us the need of a Saviour, enable us to believe in Christ, explain to us the Scriptures, and help us in our preaching. It was my beginning to understand this latter point in particular, which had a great effect on me; for the Lord enabled me to put it to the test of experience, by laying aside commentaries, and almost every other book, and simply reading the Word of God and studying it.

The result of this was that the first evening I shut myself into my room to give myself to prayer and meditation over the Scriptures. I learned more in a few hours than I had done during a period of several months previously. *But the particular difference was that I received real strength for my soul in doing so.* I now began to try by the test of the Scriptures the things which I had learned and seen, and found that only those principles which stood the test were really of value (N1, 1829).

Election: not a devilish doctrine . . .

Before this period I had been much opposed to the
doctrines of election, particular redemption, and final
persevering grace; so much so that, a few days after my
arrival at Teignmouth, I called election a devilish doctrine.
I did not believe that I had brought myself to the Lord, for
that was too manifestly false; but yet I held that I might
have finally resisted.

And further, I knew nothing about the choice of God's
people, and did not believe that the child of God, when
once made so, was safe for ever. In my fleshly mind I had
repeatedly said, 'If once I could prove that I am a child of
God for ever, I might go back into the world for a year or
two, and then return to the Lord, and at last be saved.'

But now I was brought to examine these precious truths
by the Word of God. Being made willing to have no glory of
my own in the conversion of sinners, but to consider myself
merely as an instrument; and being made willing to receive
what the Scriptures said, I went to the Word, reading the
New Testament from the beginning with a particular
reference to these truths. To my great astonishment I found
that the passages which speak decidedly for election and
persevering grace were about four times as many as those
which speak apparently against these truths; and even
those few, shortly after, when I had examined and understood them, served to confirm me in the above doctrines
(N1, 1829).

. . . the means of producing holiness

As to the effect which my belief in these doctrines had on
me, I must say, for God's glory, that though I am still
exceedingly weak, and by no means so dead to the lusts of

the flesh, and the lust of the eyes, and the pride of life, as I might and as I ought to be, yet, by the grace of God, I have walked more closely with Him since that period. My life has not been so variable, and I may say that I have lived much more for God than before. And for this have I been strengthened by the Lord, in a great measure, through understanding these truths.

For in the time of temptation, I have been repeatedly led to say, 'Should I thus sin? I should only bring misery into my soul for a time, and dishonour God; for being a son of God for ever, I should have to be brought back again, though it might be in the way of severe chastisement.'

Thus I say, the electing love of God in Christ (when I have been able to realise it) has often been the means of *producing holiness, instead of leading me into sin*. It is only the notional appreciation of such truths, not having them in the heart, whilst they are in the head, which is dangerous (N1, 1829).

The hope of the Church

Another truth into which, in a measure, I was led during my stay in Devonshire concerned the Lord's coming. My views concerning this point had, up to that time, been vague and unscriptural. I had believed what others told me, without trying it by the Word.

I thought that things were getting better and better, and that soon the whole world would be converted. But now I found in the Word that we have not the least scriptural warrant to look for the conversion of the world before the return of our Lord. I found in the Scriptures that that which will usher in the glory of the Church, and uninterrupted joy to the saints, is the return of the Lord Jesus, and that, till then, things will be more or less in confusion.

I found in the Word, that the return of Jesus, and not death, was the hope of the apostolic Christians; and that it became me therefore to look for His appearing. And this truth entered so into my heart, that, though I went into Devonshire exceedingly weak, scarcely expecting that I should return again to London, yet I was immediately, on seeing this truth, brought off from looking for death, and was made to look for the return of the Lord. Having seen this truth, the Lord enabled me to apply it, in some measure at least, to my own heart, and to put the solemn question to myself, 'What may I do for the Lord, before He returns, as He may soon come?' (N1, 1829).

Joyful communion with God

After my return to London [from a summer convalescing in Devon], I sought to benefit my brethren in the seminary, and the means which I used were these. I proposed to them to meet together every morning from six to eight for prayer and reading the Scriptures, and that then each of us should share what he might consider the Lord had shown him to be the meaning of the portion read.

One brother in particular was brought into the same state as myself; and others I trust were more or less benefited. Several times, when I went to my room after family prayer in the evening, I found communion with God so sweet, that I continued in prayer till twelve, and then, being full of joy, went into the room of the brother just referred to; and, finding him also in a similar frame of heart, we continued praying until one or two; and even then I was a few times so full of joy, that I could scarcely sleep, and at six in the morning again called the brethren together for prayer (N1, 1829).

A bad start to Christmas day

On December 24, 1829, I went to the Church Missionary Institution at Islington, in the hope of benefiting the students there, if it were the Lord's will. I returned very happy, as I almost invariably was at that time, and went to bed full of joy.

Next morning, (being that of Christmas day), I awoke in a very different state of heart from what I had experienced for many weeks past. I had no enjoyment and felt cold and lifeless in prayer. At our usual morning meeting, however, one of the brethren persuaded me to continue to pray, saying that the Lord surely would again smile on me, though now for a season, for wise purposes, He seemed to have withdrawn Himself.

I did so. At the Lord's table in the morning, a measure of enjoyment gradually returned. Towards evening the Lord gave me an opportunity of speaking about His return, and I had great enjoyment in doing so. At eight o'clock I was asked to expound at family prayer, and was much assisted by the Lord. About half an hour after the exposition was over, I was requested to come out of the room to see one of the servants, and the mother of another of the servants, who had been present at family prayer. I found them in tears, and both deeply impressed and under concern about their souls. I then went home at least as happy as on the previous evening.

I have related this, because I am aware that it is a common temptation of Satan to make us give up the reading of the Word and prayer when our enjoyment is gone; as if it were of no use to read the Scriptures when we do not enjoy them, and as if it were of no use to pray when we have no spirit of prayer. The truth is that, in order to enjoy the Word, we ought to continue to read it, and the way to obtain a spirit of prayer is to continue praying. For the less we read the Word of God, the less we desire to read it, and the less we pray, the less we desire to pray (N1, 1829).

Believers' baptism . . .

About the beginning of April I went to preach at Sidmouth. While I was staying there, three sisters in the Lord had, in my presence, a conversation about baptism. One of them had been baptised after she had believed. After they had conversed a little on the subject, I was asked to give my opinion concerning it. I replied, 'I do not think I need to be baptised again'.

I was then asked by the sister who had been baptised, 'But have you been baptised?'

I answered, 'Yes, when I was a child.'

She then replied, 'Have you ever read the Scriptures, and prayed with reference to this subject?'

I answered, 'No.'

Then, she said, 'I beg you never to speak any more about it until you have done so.'

The Lord showed me the importance of this remark. For, while at that very time I was exhorting everyone to receive nothing which could not be proved by the Word of God, I had repeatedly spoken against believers' baptism, without having ever earnestly examined the Scriptures, or prayed concerning it. Now I determined, if God would help me, to examine that subject also, and if infant baptism were found to be scriptural, I would earnestly defend it; and if believers' baptism were right, I would as strenuously defend that, and be baptised (N1, 1830).

. . . objections considered

As soon as I had time, I set about examining the subject. The mode I adopted was as follows: I repeatedly asked God to teach me concerning it, and I read the New Testament from the beginning with particular reference to this point. But now, when I earnestly set about the matter, a number of objections presented themselves to my mind.

First, since many holy and enlightened men have been divided in opinion concerning this point, does this not prove that it is not to be expected we should come to a satisfactory conclusion about this question in the present imperfect state of the Church? This question was thus removed: if this ordinance is revealed in the Bible, why may I not know it, as the Holy Spirit is the teacher in the Church of Christ now as well as formerly?

Second, there have been but few of my friends baptised, and the greater part of them are opposed to believers' baptism, and they will turn their backs on me. Answer: though all men should forsake me, if the Lord Jesus takes me up, I shall be happy.

Third, you will be sure to lose half of your income if you are baptised. Answer: as long as I desire to be faithful to the Lord, He will not suffer me to want.

Fourth, people will call you a Baptist, and you will be reckoned among that body, and you cannot approve of all that is going on among them. Answer: it does not follow that I must in all points go along with all those who hold believers' baptism, although I should be baptised.

Fifth, you have been preaching for some years, and you will have thus publicly to confess that you have been in error, should you come to the conclusion that believers' baptism is right. Answer: it is much better to confess that I have been in error than to continue in it.

Sixth, even if believers' baptism should be right, yet it is now too late to attend to it, as you ought to have been baptised immediately on believing. Answer: it is better to fulfil a commandment of the Lord Jesus ever so late, than to continue in the neglect of it (N1, 1830).

. . . he makes his decision

It had pleased God to bring my mind into such a state that I was willing to carry out in my life whatever I should find in the Scriptures concerning this ordinance, either one way or the other. I could say, 'I will do His will', and it was on that account I believe that I soon saw which doctrine was of God, whether infant baptism or believers' baptism.

As soon as I was brought into this state of heart, I saw from the Scriptures that believers only are the proper subjects for baptism, and that immersion is the only true scriptural mode in which it ought to be attended to. The passage which particularly convinced me of the former is Acts 8:36–8, and of the latter, Romans 6:3–5.

Some time after, I was baptised. I had much peace in doing so, and never have I for one single moment regretted it.

Before I leave this point, I would just say a few words concerning the result of this matter, so far as it regards some of the objections which occurred to my mind when I was about to examine the Scriptures concerning baptism.

Concerning the first objection, my conviction now is that of all revealed truths not one is more clearly revealed in the Scriptures, and that the subject has only become obscured by men not having been willing to take the *Scriptures alone* to decide the point.

Second, not one of my true friends in the Lord has turned his back on me, as I supposed, and almost all of them have been themselves baptised since.

Third, though in one way I lost money in consequence of being baptised, yet the Lord did not allow me to be really a loser, even as it regards temporal things; for He made up the loss most bountifully (N1, [1837]).

He gives up his salary

For these reasons [his objection to pew-rents], I stated to the brethren [in the chapel in Teignmouth which he had been invited to pastor] at the end of October 1830, that I would for the future give up having any regular salary. After I had given my reasons for doing so, I read

Philippians 4, and told the saints that if they still had a desire to do something towards my support, by voluntary gifts, I had no objection to receive them, though ever so small, either in money or provisions.

A few days after it appeared to me that there was a better way still. For if I received personally every single gift offered in money, both my own time and that of the donors would be much taken up; and in this way also the poor might be kept from offering their pence, a privilege of which they ought not to be deprived. And some also might in this way give more than if it were not known who was the giver; so that it would still be doubtful whether the gift were given grudgingly or cheerfully.

For these reasons especially there was a box put up in the chapel, over which was written that whoever had a desire to do something towards my support might put his offering into the box.

At the same time it appeared to me right that henceforth I should ask no man, not even my beloved brethren and sisters, to help me, as I had done a few times according to their own request, as my expenses, on account of travelling much in the Lord's service, were too great to be met by my usual income. For unconsciously I had again been led in some measure to trust in an arm of flesh; going to man instead of going to the Lord. To come to this conclusion before God required more grace than to give up my salary (N1, 1830).

A few years after Müller and Craik began their work at Bethesda chapel in Bristol, they decided to remove from the building the boxes previously intended for their support.

The goodness of the Lord

In Teignmouth –

November 18, 1830. Our money was reduced to about eight shillings. When I was praying with my wife in the morning, the Lord brought to my mind the state of our purse, and I was led to ask Him for some money.

About four hours after, we were with a sister at Bishopsteignton, and she said to me, 'Do you want any money?'

'I told the brethren,' said I, 'dear sister, when I gave up my salary, that I would for the future tell the Lord only about my wants.'

She replied, 'But He has told me to give you some money. About a fortnight ago I asked Him what I should do for Him, and He told me to give you some money; and last Saturday it came again powerfully to my mind, and has not left me since. I felt it so forcibly last night, that I could not help speaking of it to Brother P.'

My heart rejoiced, seeing the Lord's faithfulness, but I thought it better not to tell her about our circumstances lest she should be influenced to give accordingly. I was also assured that if it were of the Lord, she could not but give. I therefore turned the conversation to other subjects, but when I left she gave me two guineas [£2.10]. We were full of joy on account of the goodness of the Lord (J, 1830).

As a guide to the value of money, remember that through most of the last century a farm labourer earned about ten shillings (50p) a week.

Tempted to distrust the Lord

On January 6, 7, and 8, 1831, I had repeatedly asked the Lord for money, but received none. On the evening of January 8th I left my room for a few minutes, and was then tempted to distrust the Lord. This was even though He had been so gracious to us, in that He not only up to that day had supplied all our wants, but had given us also many answers to prayer. I was so sinful for about five minutes as to think it would be of no use to trust in the Lord in this way. I also began to say to myself that perhaps I had gone too far in living in this way.

But, thanks to the Lord, this trial lasted but a few minutes. He enabled me again to trust in Him, and Satan was immediately confounded. For when I returned to my room (out of which I had not been absent ten minutes), the Lord had sent deliverance. A sister in the Lord, who lived at Exeter, had come to Teignmouth, and brought us £2 4s [£2.20]. So the Lord triumphed, and our faith was strengthened (J, 1831).

Looking neither to man nor the box

January 10, 1831. Today, when we had again but a few shillings, £5 was given to us which had been taken out of the box. I had, once for all, told the brethren who had the care of these things to have the kindness to let me have the money every week. But as these beloved brethren either forgot to take it out weekly, or were ashamed to bring it out in such small sums, it was generally taken out every three, four, or five weeks.

As I had stated to them from the commencement that I desired to look neither to man nor the box, but to the living God, I thought it not right on my part to remind them of my request to have the money weekly, lest it should hinder the testimony which I wished to give of trusting in the living God alone.

It was on this account that on January 28, when we had again but little money, though I had seen the brother on January 24 open the box and take out the money, I would not ask the brother in whose hands it was to let me have it. But standing in need of it, as our coal was almost gone, I

42

asked the Lord to incline his heart to bring it, and but a little time afterwards it was given to us, even £1 8s 6d [£1.42½] (J, 1831).

A means of keeping from anxiety

If you should think that such a mode of living leads away from the Lord, and from caring about spiritual things, and has the effect of causing the mind to be taken up with the questions like, 'What shall I eat?', 'What shall I drink?', or 'What shall I wear?', and that therefore it would be better to have a stated salary, let me say this.

First, I have had experience of both ways, and know that my present mode of living, as to material things, is connected with less care.

Second, confidence in the Lord, to whom alone I look for the supply of my material needs, keeps me, at least whilst faith is in exercise, when a case of distress comes before me, or when the Lord's work calls for my financial aid, from anxious reckoning like this: 'Will my salary last out?', or 'Shall I have enough myself next month?' In this my freedom, I am, by the grace of God, generally at least, able to say to myself something like this: 'My Lord is not limited. He can again supply. He knows that this present case has been sent to me.' Thus, this way of living, so far from *leading to anxiety*, as it regards possible future need, is rather the means of *keeping from it*.

Third, this way of living has often been the means of reviving the work of grace in my heart when I have been getting cold; and it has also been the means of bringing me back again to the Lord, after I have been backsliding. For it is not possible to live in sin, and at the same time, by communion with God, to draw down from Heaven everything one needs for this life.

Fourth, frequently a fresh answer to prayer, obtained in this way, has been the means of filling me with much joy (N1, 1831).

A sleepless night for brother Y and his wife

June 12, 1831, Sunday. On Thursday last I went with brother Craik to Torquay to preach there. I had only about 3 shillings [15p] with me, and left my wife with about 6 shillings at home. The Lord provided beds for us through the hospitality of a brother. I asked the Lord repeatedly for money. But when I came home my wife had only about 3 shillings left, having received nothing.

We waited still upon the Lord. Yesterday passed away, and no money came. We had less than a shilling left. This morning we were still waiting upon the Lord, and looking for deliverance. We had only a little butter left for breakfast, sufficient for brother E and a relative living with us, to whom we did not mention our circumstances that they might not be made uncomfortable.

After the morning meeting, brother Y most unexpectedly opened the box. On giving me, quite as unexpectedly, the money at such a time, he told me that he and his wife could not sleep last night, on account of thinking that we might want money. The most striking point is that after I had repeatedly asked the Lord, but received nothing, I then prayed yesterday that the Lord would be pleased to impress it on brother Y that we wanted money, so that he might open the box. Our joy on account of this fresh deliverance was great, and we praised the Lord heartily (J, 1831).

Faith to get up

February 18, 1832. This afternoon I broke a blood vessel in my stomach and lost a considerable quantity of blood. I was very happy immediately afterwards.

February 19. This morning, Sunday, two brethren called on me to ask what arrangements there should be made today regarding the four villages where some of the brethren were in the habit of preaching, as, on account of my not being able to preach, one of the brethren would need to stay at home to take my place. I asked them kindly to come again in about an hour, when I would give them an answer.

After they had gone, the Lord gave me faith to rise. I dressed myself, and determined to go to the chapel. I was enabled to do so, though so weak when I went that walking the short distance to the chapel was an exertion to me. I was enabled to preach this morning with as loud and strong a voice as usual, and for the usual length of time.

After the morning meeting, a medical friend called on me, and begged me not to preach again in the afternoon as it might greatly injure me. I told him that I should indeed consider it great presumption to do so, had the Lord not given me faith. I preached again in the afternoon, and this medical friend called again and said the same concerning the evening meeting. Nevertheless, having faith, I preached again in the evening.

After each meeting I became stronger, which was a plain proof that the hand of God was in the matter. After the third meeting I went immediately to bed, considering that it would be presumption to try my strength needlessly (J, 1832).

Faith as a good coin

February 20, 1832. The Lord enabled me to rise early in the morning, and to go to our usual prayer-meeting, where I read, spoke, and prayed. Afterwards I wrote four letters, expounded the Scriptures at home, and attended the meeting again in the evening.

February 21. I attended the two meetings as usual, preached in the evening, and did my other work besides.

February 22. Today I attended the meeting in the morning, walked six miles with two brethren to Newton Bushel, and rode from there to Plymouth.

February 23. I am now as well as I was before I broke the blood vessel.

In relating this circumstance I would earnestly warn you not to imitate me if you have no faith; but if you have, it will, as a good coin, certainly be honoured by God.

I could not say that, if such a thing should happen again, I would act in the same way. For when I have been not nearly so weak as when I had broken the blood vessel, having no faith, I did not preach. Yet if it were to please the Lord to give me faith, I might be able to do the same, though even still weaker than at the time just spoken of (J, 1832).

The gift and grace of faith

About this time [1832] I repeatedly prayed with sick believers till they were restored. *Unconditionally* I asked the Lord for the blessing of bodily health, (a thing which I could not do now), and almost always had the petition granted. In some instances, however, the prayer was not answered.

In the same way, whilst in London in November 1829, in answer to my prayers, I was immediately restored from an illness from which I had suffered for a long time, and which has never returned since.

The way in which I now account for these facts is as follows. It pleased the Lord, I think, to give me in such cases something like the gift (not grace) of faith, so that unconditionally I could ask and look for an answer.

The difference between the *gift* and the *grace* of faith seems to me this. According to the *gift of faith* I am able to do a thing, or believe that a thing will come to pass, the not doing of which, or the not believing of which *would not be sin*. According to the *grace of faith* I am able to do a thing or believe that a thing will come to pass, respecting which I have the Word of God as the ground to rest upon: not doing this, or not believing it *would be sin*. For instance, the *gift of faith* would be needed to believe that a sick person should be restored again though there is no human probability: for *there is no promise to that effect*. The *grace of faith* is needed to believe that the Lord will give me the necessities of life, if I first seek the kingdom of God and His righteousness: for there is a promise to that effect (Matthew 6:33), (N1, 1869).

On the Bristol coach

April 21, 1832. This morning I rose a little before five, and attended a prayer-meeting from a quarter past five to a quarter past six. I spoke for some time at the meeting. Afterwards I prayed and read again with some believers, and likewise expounded the Scriptures.

The Bristol coach picked me up about ten. I was very faithless on the journey. I did not speak a single word for Christ, and was therefore wretched in my soul. This has shown me again my weakness. The Lord had been so gracious to me yesterday, in this particular, both on my way from Teignmouth to Exeter, and from Exeter to Taleford, and had given me much encouragement in that He made my fellow-travellers either thankfully receive the Word, or constrained them quietly to listen to the testimony. Yet I did not confess Him today. Nor did I give away a single tract, though I had my pockets full on purpose. O wretched man that I am! (J, 1832).

I would offer here a word of warning to my fellow-believers. Often the work of the Lord itself may be a temptation to keep us from that communion with Him which is so essential to the benefit of our own souls.

On the 19th I had left Dartmouth, conversed a good deal that day, preached in the evening, walked afterwards eight miles, had only about five hours sleep, travelled again the next day twenty-five miles, preached twice, and conversed very much besides, went to bed at eleven, and rose before five (N1, 1832).

Too much activity

All this shows that my body and spirit required rest, and, therefore, however careless about the Lord's work I might have appeared to my brethren, I ought to have had a great deal of quiet time for prayer and reading the Word, especially as I had a long journey before me that day, and as I was going to Bristol, which in itself required much prayer.

Instead of this I hurried to the prayer-meeting after a few minutes' private prayer. But let none think that public prayer will make up for closet communion. Then again, afterwards, when I ought to have withdrawn myself, as it were, by force, from the company of beloved brethren and sisters, and given my testimony for the Lord (and, indeed, it would have been the best testimony I could have given them), by telling them that I needed secret communion with the Lord: I did not do so, but spent the time till the coach came, in conversation with them. Now however profitable it may have been in some respects to those with whom I was on that morning, yet my own soul needed food;

and not having had it, I was lean, and felt the effects of it the whole day, and thus I believe it came that I was dumb on the coach (N1, 1832).

On conviction of sin

In Bristol
October 1, 1832. A meeting for inquirers this afternoon from two to five. Many more are convinced of sin through brother Craik's preaching than my own. This circumstance led me to inquire into the reasons, which are probably these.

First, brother Craik is more spiritually minded than I am.

Second, he prays more for the conversion of sinners than I do.

Third, he more frequently addresses sinners, as such, in his preaching than I do (J, 1832).

This led me to more frequent and earnest prayer for the conversion of sinners, and to address them more frequently as such. The latter had never been intentionally left undone, but it had not been so frequently brought to my mind as to that of brother Craik. Since then, the cases in which it has pleased the Lord to use me as an instrument of conversion have been quite as many as those in which brother Craik has been used.

May the Lord be pleased to use this as a means to lead any of His servants who may not have acted according to the last two points to seek to do so, and may He graciously enable me to do so more abundantly! (N1, 1837).

Why he didn't ask unbelievers for money

The means which are made use of in [some] religious societies to obtain money for the work of the Lord are in some respects unscriptural. It is a most common case *to ask* the *unconverted* for money. Even Abraham would not have done this (Gen. 14:21–4): and how much less should *we* do it, who are not only forbidden to have fellowship with unbelievers in these matters (2 Cor. 6:14–18), but who are also in fellowship with the Father and the Son, and can therefore obtain everything from the Lord which we can possibly need in His service. How altogether differently the first disciples acted in this respect we learn from 3 John 7 . . . (N1, 1834).

Extract from the principles of the Scriptural Knowledge Institution for Home and Abroad which he and Henry Craik established in March 1834 and which still flourishes –

We do not mean to *ask* unbelievers for money (2 Cor. 6:14–18); though we do not feel ourselves warranted to refuse their contributions if they of their own accord should offer them (Acts 28:2–10), (N1, 1834).

Enjoying a nearness to God

During a time of illness –

September 27, 1835. Today I am thirty years of age. I feel myself an unprofitable servant. How much more might I have lived for God than I have done! May the Lord grant that if I am allowed to stay a few more days in this world, they may be spent entirely for Him!

September 29. Last evening, when I retired from the family, I had a desire to go to rest at once, for I had prayed a short while before; and feeling weak in body, the coldness of the night was a temptation for me to pray no further. However the Lord did help me to fall upon my knees; and no sooner had I commenced praying than He shone into my soul, and gave me such a spirit of prayer as I had not enjoyed for many weeks. He graciously once more revived His work in my heart. I enjoyed that nearness to God and fervency in prayer for more than an hour for which my soul had been panting for many weeks past.

For the first time during this illness, I now had also a spirit of prayer regarding my health. I could ask the Lord earnestly to restore me again, which had not been the case before. I now long earnestly to go back to Bristol, yet without impatience, and feel assured that the Lord will strengthen me to return to it. I went to bed especially happy and awoke this morning in great peace, rose sooner than usual, and had again for more than an hour real communion with the Lord before breakfast. May He in mercy continue this state of heart to His most unworthy child! (J, 1835).

Why he established an orphan house . . .

Through my pastoral labours among the saints in Bristol, through my considerable correspondence, and through brethren who visited Bristol, I constantly had cases brought before me which proved that one of the special things which the children of God needed in our day was to *have their faith strengthened*.

For instance: I might visit a brother who worked fourteen or even sixteen hours a day at his trade. The result of this was that not only his body suffered, but his soul was lean, and he had no enjoyment in the things of God. Under such circumstances I might point out to him that he ought to work less, in order that his bodily health might not suffer, and that he might gather strength for his inner man by reading the Word of God, by meditation over it and by prayer.

The reply however I generally found to be something like this: 'But if I work less, I do not earn enough for the support of my family. Even now, whilst I work so much, I have scarcely enough. The wages are so low, that I must work hard in order to obtain what I need.'

There was no trust in God. No real belief in the truth of that word: 'Seek first the Kingdom of God, and all these things shall be added unto you' (Matt. 6:33 AV).

I might reply something like this: 'My dear brother, it is not your work which supports your family, but the Lord. And He who has fed you and your family when you could not work at all, on account of illness, would surely provide for you and yours, if, for the sake of obtaining food for your inner man, you were to work only so many hours a day as would allow you proper time for retirement. And is it not the case now that you begin the work of the day after having had only a few hurried moments for prayer; and when you leave off your work in the evening, and mean then to read a little of the Word of God, are you not too much worn out in body and mind to enjoy it? Do you not often fall asleep whilst reading the Scriptures, or whilst on your knees in prayer?'

The brother would allow that it was so; he would allow that my advice was good; but still I read in his countenance, even if he should not have actually said so, 'How should I get on, if I were to *carry out* your advice?' (N1, 1835).

. . . the visible proof

I longed, therefore, to have something to point the brother to, as a visible proof that our God and Father is the same faithful God as ever He was; as willing as ever to prove Himself to be the living God, in our day as formerly, to all who put their trust in Him.

Sometimes, I found brethren in business who suffered in their souls, and brought guilt on their consciences, by carrying on their business almost in the same way as unconverted persons do. The competition in trade, the bad times, the over-peopled country, were given as reasons why, if the business were carried on simply according to the Word of God, it could not be expected to do well. Such a brother, perhaps, would express the wish that he might be differently situated. But very rarely did I see *that there was a stand made for God, that there was the holy determination to trust in the living God, and to depend on Him, in order that a good conscience might be maintained*. To such people also I desired to show, by a visible proof, that God is unchangeably the same.

My spirit longed to be instrumental in strengthening their faith, by giving them not only instances from the Word of God of His willingness and ability to help all those who rely upon Him, but *to show them by proofs*, that He is the same in our day.

I well knew *that the Word of God ought to be enough*, and it was, by grace, enough for me; but still, I considered that I ought to lend a helping hand to my brethren, if by this visible proof to the unchangeable faithfulness of the Lord, I might strengthen their hands in God. I remembered what a great blessing my own soul had received through the Lord's dealings with His servant A.H. Franke, who, in dependence on the living God alone, established an immense orphan house which I had seen many times with my own eyes (N1, 1835).

August Franke (1663–1727) established free schools and an orphan house in Halle in the closing years of the seventeenth century.

. . . the reality of the things of God

I therefore judged myself bound to be the servant of the Church of Christ in the particular point on which I had obtained mercy: namely, *in being able to take God by His*

Word and to rely upon it. All these exercises of my soul resulted from the fact that so many believers with whom I became acquainted were harassed and distressed in mind, or brought guilt on their consciences, on account of not trusting in the Lord. This was used by God to awaken in my heart the desire of setting before the Church at large, and before the world, a proof that He has not in the least changed; and this seemed to me best done by establishing an orphan house. It needed to be something which could be seen, even by the natural eye.

Now if I a poor man, simply by prayer and faith, obtained *without asking any individual,* the means for establishing and carrying on an orphan house: there would be something which, with the Lord's blessing, might be instrumental in strengthening the faith of the children of God, besides being a testimony to the consciences of the unconverted, of the reality of the things of God.

This, then, was the primary reason for establishing the orphan house. I certainly did from my heart desire to be used by God to benefit the bodies of poor children, bereaved of both parents, and seek, in other respects, with the help of God, to do them good for this life. I also particularly longed to be used by God in getting the dear orphans trained up in the fear of God. But still, the first and primary object of the work was (and still is): that God might be magnified by the fact that the orphans under my care are provided with all they need only *by prayer and faith,* without anyone being asked by me or my fellow-labourers. In this way, it may be seen that God is faithful still, and hears prayer still (N1, 1835/69).

Speaking out of the full heart

May 7, 1838. This morning I left Leamington for Bristol. I had grace to confess the Lord Jesus the last part of the way before several merry passengers, and had the honour of being ridiculed for His sake. There are few things in which I feel more entirely dependent upon the Lord, than in confessing Him on such occasions. Sometimes I have, by grace, had much real boldness; but often I have shown the greatest weakness, doing no more than refraining entirely from unholy conversation, without speaking a single word for Him who toiled beyond measure for me.

No other remedy do I know for myself and any of my fellow-saints who are weak, like myself, in this respect, than to seek to have the heart so full of Jesus, and to live so in the realisation of what He has done for us, that, without any effort, out of the full heart, we may speak for Him.

I found my dear family in peace (J, 1838).

The unchangeableness of our adorable Lord

July 22, 1838. This evening I was walking in our little garden, meditating on Hebrews 13:8, 'Jesus Christ is the same yesterday and today, and for ever.' Whilst meditating on His unchangeable love, power and wisdom, and turning all as I went into prayer respecting myself; and whilst applying also His unchangeable love, power, and wisdom both to my present spiritual and temporal circumstances – all at once the present need of the orphan houses was brought to my mind.

Immediately I was led to say to myself, 'Jesus in His love and power has hitherto supplied me with what I have needed for the orphans, and in the same unchangeable love and power He will provide me with what I may need for the future.'

A flow of joy came into my soul whilst realising thus the unchangeableness of our adorable Lord. About one minute after, a letter was brought me enclosing a cheque for twenty pounds. In it was written: 'Will you apply the amount of the enclosed cheque to the objects of your Scriptural Knowledge Society, or of your Orphan Establishment, or in the work and cause of our Master in any way that He Himself, on your application to Him, may point out to you. It is not a great sum, but it is a sufficient provision for the exigency of today; and it is for *today's* exigencies that ordinarily the Lord provides. Tomorrow, as it brings its demands, will find its supply' (J, 1838).

A longer way home

November 21, 1838. Never were we so reduced in funds as today. There was not a single halfpenny in hand between the matrons of the three houses. Nevertheless there was a good dinner, and, by managing to help one another with bread, etc., there was a prospect of getting over this day also; but for none of the houses had we the prospect of being able to take in bread.

When I left the brethren and sisters at one o'clock, after prayer, I told them that we must wait for help, and see how the Lord would deliver us at this time. I was sure of help, but we were indeed straitened.

When I came to Kingsdown, I felt that I needed more exercise, being very cold; wherefore I went not the nearest way home, but round by Clarence Place. About twenty yards from my house, I met a brother who walked back with me, and after a little conversation gave me ten pounds to be handed over to the deacons, towards providing the poor saints with coal, blankets and warm clothing; also five pounds for the orphans, and five pounds for the other objects of the Scriptural Knowledge Institution.

The brother had called twice while I was at the orphan houses, and had I now been *one half minute* later, I should have missed him. But the Lord knew our need, and therefore allowed me to meet him. I sent off the five pounds immediately to the matrons (J, 1838).

Laying the case in simplicity before the Lord . . .

November 28, 1838. This is perhaps of all days the most remarkable as yet, so far as it regards the funds. When I was in prayer this morning respecting them, I was enabled firmly to believe that the Lord would send help, though all seemed dark as to natural appearances. At twelve o'clock I met as usual with the brethren and sisters for prayer. There had come in only one shilling (5p), which was left last evening anonymously at the infant orphan house, and which except for two pennies had already been spent on account of our great need.

I heard also that an individual had cleaned the clock in the infant orphan house at no charge, and had offered to keep the clocks in the three houses in repair. Thus the Lord gave even in this a little encouragement, and a proof that He is still mindful of us.

On inquiry I found that there was everything needful for the lunch in all the three houses; but neither in the infant nor boys' orphan houses was there bread enough for tea, nor money to buy milk. Lower had we never been, and perhaps never so low.

We gave ourselves unitedly to prayer, laying the case in simplicity before the Lord . . . (J, 1838).

. . . He sends help

November 28, 1838 (cont.) . . . Whilst in prayer there was a knock at the door, and one of the sisters went out. After the two brethren, who labour in the orphan houses, and I had prayed aloud we continued for a while silently in prayer.

As to myself, I was lifting up my heart to the Lord to make a way of escape, and in order to know if there were any other thing which I could do with a good conscience, besides waiting on Him, so that we might have food for the children.

At last we rose from our knees.

I said, 'God will surely send help.'

The words had not quite passed over my lips when I saw a letter lying on the table which had been brought while we were in prayer. It was from my wife, containing another letter from a brother with ten pounds for the orphans. The evening before last I was asked by a brother whether the balance in hand for the orphans would be as great this time when the accounts would be made up as last time. My answer was that it would be as great as the Lord pleased.

The next morning this brother was moved to remember the orphans, and to send today ten pounds, which arrived after I left my house, and which on account of our need had been forwarded immediately to me. Thus I was enabled to give six pounds ten shillings for housekeeping, and to put by three pounds ten shillings for rent.

The brother who sent the ten pounds for the orphans, also sent ten pounds to be divided between brother Craik and me, with the object of purchasing new clothes for ourselves (J, 1838).

A bank which cannot break

February 13, 1839. Since February 8, five donations amounting to nine pounds nine shillings had come in. This afternoon I paid out the last money which we had in hand, and in giving it to brother T. said, 'We have now again to look to the Lord for further supplies.'

This evening five pounds was given to me, which had come in the following way. A gentleman and lady visited the orphan houses, and met at the boys' orphan house two ladies who were also visiting.

One of the ladies said to the matron of the boys' orphan house, 'Of course you cannot carry on these institutions without a good stock of funds.'

The gentleman, turning to the matron, said, 'Have you a good stock?'

She replied, 'Our funds are deposited in a bank which cannot break.'

Tears came into the eyes of the inquiring lady. The gentleman, on leaving, gave to the master of the boys five pounds, which came in *when I had not a penny in hand* (J, 1839).

A heart, a cross and roses

February 3, 1840. Today I left Bristol for Berlin . . . We landed at Hamburg on the 7th at five in the afternoon. The porter who carried my things led me, as I afterwards found out, some by-way, either to save a long distance, or to get me into the city with my luggage, though it was after the custom-house hours. I did not understand this at first; but, when we were about to enter the city, he told me that that was not the proper way, but that if I would give to the custom-house officer, whom I should see at the entrance into the city, a small fee, he would let me pass.

My reply was that I did not wish to do that which was unlawful, nor should I give a fee to encourage that which was unlawful. I would rather go a long way round, than get by such means into the city.

Presently we arrived at the place at which the custom-house officer stood, who, on my telling him plainly that I had not the least wish to pass that way, if it were unlawful, saw that I was only a passenger, and that I had no wish to go into the city with goods which are not duty free, and therefore let me pass.

This little circumstance proves afresh in how many little things the children of God may act differently from the world, to the glory of their Father, and how in going the Lord's way, we find it to be, even as far as this life is concerned, the easiest path.

About half an hour after, when I arrived at the hotel, a little circumstance served afresh to remind me, that the Christian, like the bee, might suck honey out of every flower. I saw upon a snuffer-stand in bas-relief, 'A heart, a cross under it, and roses under both.' The meaning was obviously this, that the heart which bears the cross for a time meets with roses afterwards. I applied it to myself, and this little event greatly cheered my heart in this place, where I was without the fellowship of a single believer (J, 1840).

Giving up his own will

In Germany –

I had travelled so fast, and stayed so short a time in the places where I had been, that I was obliged to leave Heimersleben without having received the letter which I had expected from my wife. This was a matter of no small trial – as those who have been for some time at a great distance from home know. This was especially so in my case, as, on account of the orphans and the other work, besides my family, it was of so much importance for me to hear from time to time.

I had arranged with my father to have the letter sent to

me to Sandersleben, by an express messenger, who could be obtained for a small fee. However, hour after hour passed away and the messenger still did not arrive. At last the time was gone by, as it was getting dark, and the person ought to have come at noon. I now lifted up my heart to the Lord, beseeching Him to give me grace to give up my own will in this thing. *No sooner had I been brought into such a state, as to be truly content and satisfied with the will of the Lord in this matter*, than the expected letter was handed over to me.

The woman who brought it had lost her way in the morning, on account of a dense fog, which made her so late. I have frequently found, under similar circumstances, that after I had been brought into such a state as to be willing to give up my own will, whereby I was fitted to bear the blessing, the Lord gave me the desire of my heart, according to the truth of that word: 'Delight yourself in the Lord and he will give you the desires of your heart' (Ps. 37:4), (J, 1840).

Jehovah Jireh

November 8, 1840, Sunday. Today the Lord has been again very kind, and looked upon us in our poverty. Besides the one pound ten shillings for rent, I received with Ecclesiastes 9:10, five pounds. I was informed that two large sacks of oatmeal had been sent from Glasgow as a present.

In addition to all this, a brother told me that he had it in his heart to give ten pounds worth of materials for winter clothes for the children, leaving the material to my choice, according to the need, so that just what was most desirable might be given. (He accordingly sent a few days after a large pair of good blankets, 32½ yards of mixed beaver, and 10½ yards of blue beaver for cloaks.) There was also one shilling put into the box at Bethesda, with the words, 'Jehovah Jireh' (J, 1840).

These words have often been refreshing to my soul for many years past, and I wrote them with a valuable diamond ring, set with ten brilliants, which was given for the orphans about twenty months ago, upon a pane of glass in my room, which circumstance, in remembrance of the remarkable way in which that valuable ring came, has often cheered my heart, *when in deep poverty my eyes have been cast upon* 'JEHOVAH JIREH' (the Lord will provide) whilst sitting in my room (N1, 1840).

Bringing the Lord remarkably near

This way of living brings the Lord remarkably near. He is, as it were, morning by morning inspecting our stores, that accordingly He may send help. Greater and more manifest nearness of the Lord's presence I have never had, than when after breakfast there were no means for lunch, and then the Lord provided the lunch for more than one hundred persons; or when, after lunch, there were no means for the tea, and yet the Lord provided the tea; and all this without one single human being having been informed about our need.

This moreover I add, that although we, who have been eye witnesses of these gracious interventions of our Father have not been so benefited by them as we might and ought to have been, yet we have in some measure derived blessings from them.

One thing is certain, that we are not tired of doing the Lord's work in this way (N1, 1840).

To those who work with children

As far as my experience goes, it appears to me that believers generally have expected far too little of *present* fruit upon their labours among children. There has been a hoping that the Lord some day or other would own the instruction which they give to children, and would answer at some time or other, though after many years only, the prayers which they offer up on their behalf.

Now such passages as Proverbs 12:6, Ecclesiastes 11:1, Galatians 6:9, and 1 Corinthians 15:58 give us assurance not merely respecting everything we do for the Lord in general, but also respecting bringing up children in the fear of the Lord in particular, that our labour is not in vain in the Lord. However we have to guard against abusing such passages by thinking it a matter of little moment whether we see *present* fruit or not. We should in fact give the Lord no rest till we see present fruit, and therefore in persevering, yet submissive, prayer we should make known our requests unto God.

I add, as an encouragement to believers who labour among children, that during the last two years, seventeen or more young persons or children, from the age of eleven and a half to seventeen, have been received into fellowship among us. I am looking out now for many more to be converted, and that not merely of the orphans, but of the Sunday and day school children. As in so many respects we are living in remarkable times, so in this respect also, the Lord is working greatly among children in many places (N1, 1840).

The first business of the day

While I was staying at Nailsworth [Gloucestershire], it pleased the Lord to teach me a truth, irrespective of human instrumentality, as far as I know, the benefit of which I have not lost, though now, whilst preparing the seventh edition for the press [1869], more than twenty-seven years have passed away.

The point is this: I saw more clearly than ever, that the first great and primary business to which I ought to attend every day was to have my soul happy in the Lord. The first thing to be concerned about was not how much I might serve the Lord, how I might glorify the Lord; but how I might get my soul into a happy state, and how my inner man might be nourished.

For I might seek to set the truth before the unconverted, I might seek to benefit believers, I might seek to relieve the distressed, I might in other ways seek to behave myself as it becomes a child of God in this world; and yet, not being happy in the Lord, and not being nourished and strengthened in my inner man day by day, all this might not be attended to in a right spirit.

Before this time my practice had been, at least for ten years previously, as an habitual thing, to give myself to prayer, after having dressed myself in the morning. *Now* I saw that the most important thing I had to do was to give myself to the reading of the Word of God and to meditation on it, that thus my heart might be comforted, encouraged, warned, reproved, instructed; and that thus, by means of the Word of God, whilst meditating on it, my heart might be brought into experimental communion with the Lord (N1, 1841).

Food for my own soul

I began therefore to meditate on the New Testament from the beginning early in the morning. The first thing I did, after having asked in a few words the Lord's blessing upon

64

His precious Word, was to begin to meditate on the Word of God, searching as it were into every verse to get blessing out of it; not for the sake of the public ministry of the Word; not for the sake of preaching on what I had meditated upon, but for the sake of obtaining food for my own soul.

The result I have found to be almost invariably this, that after a very few minutes my soul has been led to confession, or to thanksgiving, or to intercession, or to supplication; so that, though I did not, as it were give myself to *prayer*, but to *meditation*, yet it turned almost immediately more or less into prayer. When thus I have been for a while making confession, or intercession, or supplication, or have given thanks, I go on to the next words or verse, turning all as I go on into prayer for myself or others, as the Word may lead to it; but still continually keeping before me, that food for my own soul is the object of my meditation.

The result of this is that there is always a good deal of confession, thanksgiving, supplication, or intercession mingled with my meditation, and that my inner man almost invariably is sensibly nourished and strengthened, and that by breakfast time, with rare exceptions, I am in a peaceful if not happy state of heart.

Thus also the Lord is pleased to communicate unto me that which either very soon after, or at a later time, I have found to become food for other believers, though it was not for the sake of the public ministry of the Word that I gave myself to meditation, but for the profit of my own inner man (N1, 1841).

Experimental fellowship with God

With this mode I have also combined being out in the open air for an hour, an hour and a half, or two hours before breakfast, walking about in the fields, and in the summer sitting for a while on the stiles, if I find it too much to walk

65

all the time. I find it very beneficial to my health to walk thus for meditation before breakfast, and am now so in the habit of using the time for that purpose, that when I get into the open air, I generally take out a New Testament of good sized type, which I carry with me for that purpose, besides my Bible: and I find that I can profitably spend my time in the open air, which formerly was not the case for want of habit.

I used to consider the time spent in walking a loss, but now I find it very profitable, not only to my body, but also to my soul. The walking out before breakfast is of course not necessarily connected with this matter, and everyone has to judge according to his strength and other circumstances.

The difference then between my former practice and my present one is this. Formerly when I rose, I began to pray as soon as possible, and generally spent all my time till breakfast in prayer, or almost all the time. What was the result? I often spent a quarter of an hour, or half an hour, or even an hour on my knees, before being conscious to myself of having derived comfort, encouragement, or humbling of soul. Often, after having suffered much from wandering of mind for the first ten minutes, or quarter of an hour, or even half an hour, I only then began *really to pray*.

I scarcely ever suffer now in this way. For my heart being nourished by the truth, being brought into *experimental* fellowship with God, I speak to my Father, and to my Friend (vile though I am, and unworthy of it!) about the things that He has brought before me in His precious Word (N1, 1841).

Strengthening the inner man

It often now astonishes me that I did not sooner see this point. In no book did I ever read about it. No public ministry ever brought the matter before me. No private conversation with a brother stirred me up to this matter. And yet now, since God has taught me this point, it is as plain to me as anything that the first thing the child of God has to do morning by morning is to *obtain food for his inner man*.

As the outward man is not fit for work for any length of time except we take food, and this is one of the first things we do in the morning, so it should be with the inner man. We should take food for that as everyone must allow. Now what is the food for the inner man? Not *prayer*, but *the Word of God*; and here again not the simple reading of the Word of God, so that it only passes through our minds, just as water runs through a pipe, but considering what we read, pondering over it, and applying it to our hearts.

When we pray we speak to God. Now prayer, in order to be continued for any length of time in any other than a formal manner, requires, generally speaking, a measure of strength or godly desire. Therefore the time when we can best perform this exercise of the soul is after the inner man has been nourished by meditation on the Word of God. This is when we find our Father speaking to us, to encourage us, to comfort us, to instruct us, to humble us, or to reprove us.

We may therefore profitably meditate, with God's blessing, though we are ever so weak spiritually; indeed the weaker we are, the more we need meditation for the strengthening of our inner man. There is thus far less to be feared from wandering of mind than if we give ourselves to prayer without having had previously time for meditation (N1, 1841).

In every believer

Do not think that I have *the gift of faith*, that is the gift of which we read in 1 Corinthians 12:9, and which is mentioned along with 'the gift of healing', 'the working of miracles', and 'prophecy', and that on that account I am able to trust in the Lord. *It is true* that the faith which I am enabled to exercise is altogether God's own gift; it is true that He alone supports it, and that He alone can increase it; it is true that moment by moment I depend upon Him for it, and that if I were only one moment left to myself my faith would utterly fail. But *it is not true* that my faith is that gift of faith which is spoken of in 1 Corinthians 12:9.

The faith which I am enabled to exercise with reference to the orphan houses, and my own material needs, is not that 'faith' of which it is said in 1 Corinthians 13:2 (evidently in allusion to the faith spoken of in 1 Corinthians 12:9), 'a faith that can move mountains'. It is the self-same faith which is found in *every believer*, and the growth of which I am most sensible of to myself; for, by little and little, it has been increasing for the last forty-three years (N1, 1842/69).

Faith in the Word and character of God

This faith which is exercised respecting the orphan houses, and my own material needs, also shows itself in the following ways. I have never been allowed to doubt during the last forty-three years that my sins are forgiven, that I am a child of God, that God loves me, and that I shall be finally saved. This is because I am enabled, by the grace of God, to exercise faith upon the Word of God, and believe what God says in those passages which settle these matters (1 John 5:1; Gal. 3:26; Acts 10:43; Rom. 10:9–10; John 3:16, etc).

When my brother in the flesh, and my dear aged father died, and when concerning both of them I had no *evidence* whatever that they were saved (though I dare not say that they are lost, for I know it not); yet my soul was at peace, perfectly at peace, under this great trial, this exceedingly great trial, this trial which is one of the greatest perhaps which can befall a believer. And what was it that gave me peace? My soul laid hold on that word, 'Shall not the judge of all the earth do right?' This word, together with the whole character of God, as He has revealed Himself in His holy Word, settled all questionings. I believed what He has said concerning Himself, and I was at peace, and have been at peace ever since, concerning this matter (N1, 1842/69).

Encouraging himself in God

When the Lord took from me a beloved infant [in 1835 the Müllers' son Elijah died of pneumonia, aged fifteen months], my soul was at peace, perfectly at peace; I could only weep tears of joy when I did weep. And why? Because my soul laid hold on that word: 'The kingdom of heaven belongs to such as these' (Matt. 19.14). Believing therefore as I did upon the ground of this word, my soul rejoiced, instead of mourning, that my beloved infant was far happier with the Lord, than with me.

When sometimes all has been dark, exceedingly dark, with reference to my service among the saints, judging from natural appearances; when I should have been overwhelmed indeed in grief and despair, had I looked at things after the outward appearance – at such times I have sought to encourage myself in God, by laying hold in faith on His mighty power, His unchangeable love, and His infinite wisdom, and I have said to myself: 'God is able and willing to deliver me if it be good for me; for it is written, "He who did not spare his own son, but gave him up for us all – how will he not also, along with him, graciously give us all things?"' (Rom. 8:32).

This it was which, being believed by me through grace, kept my soul in peace (N1, 1842).

No particular gift of faith

When in connection with the orphan houses and day schools, trials have come upon me which were far heavier than the want of means; when lying reports were spread that the orphans had not enough to eat, or that they were cruelly treated in other respects, and the like; or when other trials, still greater, but which I cannot mention, have befallen me in connection with this work, and that at a time when I was nearly a thousand miles from Bristol, and had to remain absent week after week: at such times my soul was stayed upon God; I believed His word of promise which was applicable to such cases; I poured out my soul before God, and arose from my knees in peace, because the trouble that was in the soul was in believing prayer cast upon God, and thus I was kept in peace, though I saw it to be the will of God to remain far away from the work.

When I needed houses, fellow-labourers, masters and mistresses for the orphans or for the day schools, I have been enabled to look for all to the Lord, and trust in Him for help.

I may seem to boast; but, by the grace of God, I do not boast in thus speaking. From my inmost soul I do ascribe it to God alone that He has enabled me to trust in Him, and that hitherto He has not suffered my confidence in Him to fail. But I thought it needful to make these remarks, lest anyone should think that my depending upon God was a particular gift given to me, which other saints have no right to look for; or lest it should be thought that this my depending upon Him had *only to do with the obtaining of money by prayer and faith*.

By the grace of God I desire that my faith in God should extend towards everything, the smallest of my own temporal and spiritual concerns and those of my family, towards the saints among whom I labour, the Church at large, and everything that has to do with the temporal and spiritual prosperity of the Scriptural Knowledge Institution (N1, 1842/69).

Expecting an answer

Do not think that I have attained in faith (and how much less in other respects!) to that degree to which I might and ought to attain; but thank God for the faith which He has given me. Don't let Satan deceive you in making you think that you could not have the same faith, but that it is only for persons who are situated as I am.

When I lose such a thing as a key, I ask the Lord to direct me to it, and look for an answer to my prayer; when a person with whom I have made an appointment does not come at the fixed time, and I begin to be inconvenienced by it, I ask the Lord to be pleased to hasten him to me, and I look for an answer; when I do not understand a passage from the Word of God, I lift up my heart to the Lord that He would be pleased by His Holy Spirit to instruct me, and I expect to be taught – though I do not fix the time when, and the manner how it should be.

When I am going to minister in the Word, I seek help from the Lord, and while I in the consciousness of natural inability as well as utter unworthiness, begin this service, I am not cast down, but of good cheer, because I look for His assistance, and believe that He, for His dear Son's sake will help me.

And thus in other of my concerns I pray to the Lord, and expect an answer to my requests; and may not *you* do the same, dear believing reader? (N1, 1842).

How your faith may be strengthened . . .

Do not think of me as an extraordinary believer, having privileges above other of God's dear children, which they cannot have; nor look on my way of acting as something that would not do for other believers. Make but trial! Do but stand still in the hour of trial, and you will see the help of God, if you trust in Him.

But there is so often a forsaking the ways of the Lord in the hour of trial, and thus the *food of faith*, the means by which our faith may be increased, is lost. This leads me to the following important point. You ask, 'How may I, a true believer, have my faith strengthened?'

The answer is this: 'Every good and perfect gift is from above, coming down from the Father of the heavenly lights, who does not change like shifting shadows' James 1:17. As the increase of faith is a good gift, it must come from God, and therefore He ought to be asked for this blessing. The following means however ought to be used . . . (N1, 1842).

. . . Knowing the nature and character of God

First, *the careful reading of the Word of God, combined with meditation on it*. Through the reading of the Word of God, and especially through meditation on it, the believer becomes more and more acquainted with the nature and character of God. He sees more and more, besides His holiness and justice, what a kind, loving, gracious, merciful, mighty, wise, and faithful being He is. Then in poverty, illness, bereavement, difficulty in his service, unemployment, he will repose on the *ability* of God to help him. This is because he has not only learned from His Word that He is of almighty power and infinite wisdom, but he has also seen instance upon instance in the Holy Scriptures in which His almighty power and infinite wisdom have been actually exercised in helping and delivering His people. He will repose upon the *willingness* of God to help him, because he has not only learned from the Scriptures what a kind, good, merciful, gracious, and faithful being God is, but because he has also seen in the Word of God, how in a great variety of instances He has proved Himself to be so.

And the consideration of this, if God has become known to us through prayer and meditation on His own Word, will lead us, in general at least, with a measure of confidence to rely upon Him: and thus the reading of the Word of God, together with meditation on it, will be one especial means to strengthen our faith (N1, 1842).

... Maintaining a good conscience

Second, as with reference to the growth of every grace of the Spirit, it is of the utmost importance that we seek to maintain an upright heart and good conscience. We should not knowingly and habitually indulge in those things which are contrary to the mind of God, and this is particularly the case with reference to the *growth in faith*. How can I possibly continue to put faith in God, concerning anything, if I am habitually grieving Him, and seek to detract from the glory and honour of Him in whom I profess to trust, upon whom I profess to depend?

All my confidence towards God, all my leaning upon Him in the hour of trial will be gone, if I have a guilty conscience, and do not seek to put away this guilty conscience, but still continue to do things which are contrary to the mind of God. And if, in any particular instance, I cannot trust in God because of the guilty conscience, then my faith is weakened by that instance of distrust. For faith, with every fresh trial of it, either increases by trusting God, and thus getting help, or it decreases by not trusting Him; and then there is less and less power of looking simply and directly to Him, and a habit of self dependence is encouraged. Either we trust in God, and in that case we neither trust in ourselves,

73

nor in our fellow-men, nor in circumstances, nor in anything besides; or we *do* trust in one or more of these, and in that case we do *not* trust in God (N1, 1842).

. . . Depending on Him alone

Third, if we desire our faith to be strengthened, we should not shrink from opportunities where our faith may be tried, and therefore through the trial be strengthened. In our natural state we dislike dealing with God alone. Through our natural alienation from God we shrink from Him, and from eternal realities. This cleaves to us more or less, even after our regeneration. Hence it is that, more or less, even as believers, we have the same shrinking from standing with God alone, from depending upon Him alone, from looking to Him alone: and yet this is the very position in which we ought to be, if we wish to have our faith strengthened.

The more I am in a position to be tried in faith, the more I shall have opportunity of seeing God's help and deliverance; and every fresh instance, in which He helps and delivers me, will tend towards the increase of my faith (N1, 1842).

. . . Letting God work for you

The last important point for the strengthening of our faith is that we let God work for us when the hour of the trial of our faith comes, and do not work a deliverance of our own. Wherever God has given faith, it is given, among other reasons, for the very purpose of being tried. However weak

74

our faith may be, God will try it; only with this restriction, that as, in every way, He leads on gently, gradually, patiently, so also with reference to the trial of our faith. At first our faith will be tried very little in comparison with what it may be afterwards; for God never lays more upon us than He is willing to enable us to bear.

Now when the trial of faith comes, we are naturally inclined to distrust God, and to trust rather in ourselves, or in our friends, or in circumstances. We will rather work a deliverance of our own somehow or other, than simply look to God and wait for His help. But if we do not patiently wait for God's help, if we work a deliverance of our own, then at the next trial of our faith it will be thus again, we shall be again inclined to deliver ourselves; and thus with every instance of that kind, our faith will decrease; whilst, on the contrary, were we to stand still in order to see the salvation of God, to see His hand stretched out on our behalf, our faith would be increased yet more (N1, 1842).

Writing reports – and appealing for funds

Surely all who know the Lord, and who have no interest in disowning it, cannot but see His hand in a remarkable manner in this work. Nor will the godly and simple minded reader say – 'There is no difference between this way of proceeding, on the one hand, and going from individual to individual, asking them for means, on the other hand; for the writing of reports is just the same thing.' My dear reader, there is a great difference.

Suppose we are in need. Suppose that our poverty lasts for some weeks or even some months together. Is there not, in that case, a difference between asking the Lord from day to day, without speaking to any human being not connected directly with the work about our poverty on the one hand:

and writing letters or making personal application to benevolent individuals for assistance on the other hand?

Truly, there is a great difference between these two modes. I do not mean to say that it would be acting against the precepts of the Lord to seek help in His work by personal and individual application to *believers*, (though it would be in direct opposition to His will to apply to *unbelievers*, 2 Corinthians 6:14–18); but *I* act in the way in which I do for the benefit of the Church at large, cheerfully bearing the trials, and sometimes the deep trials connected with this life of faith (which however brings along with it also great joys), if by any means a part at least of my fellow believers might be led to see the reality of dealing with God only, and that there is such a thing as the child of God having power with God by prayer and faith (N1, 1843).

Perhaps the needs are made known . . .

Should Satan seek to whisper into your ears: 'Perhaps the matter is made known after all, when there is a need' (as it has been once said about me at a public meeting at a large town, that when we were in want I prayed *publicly* that the Lord would send help for the orphans, which is entirely false), I reply, 'Whom did I ask for anything these many years since the work has been going on? To whom did I make known our wants, except to those closely connected with the work?'

No, so far from wishing to make known our need, for the purpose of influencing benevolent persons to contribute to the necessities of the institution under my care, I have even refused to let our circumstances be known, after having been asked about them, when on simply saying that we were in need, I might have had considerable sums.

In such cases I have refused, in order that the hand of

76

God only might be manifest; for that and not the money, nor even the ability of continuing to carry on the work, is my especial aim. And such self-possession has the Lord given me, that at the times of deepest poverty, (whilst there was nothing at all in hand, and whilst we had even from meal to meal to wait upon the Lord for the needs of more than one hundred persons), when a donation of five pounds or ten pounds or more has been given to me, the donors could not have read in my countenance whether we had much or nothing in hand.

But enough of this. I have made these remarks, beloved readers, lest you should lose the blessing which might come to your soul through reading the account of the Lord's faithfulness and readiness to hear the prayers of His children (N1, 1843).

The 'holy kiss'

In 1843, Müller spent over six months working in a small Baptist church in Stuttgart –

In Germany, as on the Continent generally, the kiss is the sign of affection and familiarity among men as well as women, and the brethren and sisters at Stuttgart always had been in the habit of kissing one another after having partaken of the Lord's supper – that is all the brethren had kissed each other, and all the sisters had kissed each other.

Now this again, if the result of real affection, and springing from the entering into our heavenly relationship and oneness in Christ Jesus, would be most beautiful, and would be the 'holy kiss' of which the apostle Paul speaks (1 Cor. 16:20); but I had no reason to believe this was generally the case among the brethren and sisters at Stuttgart, but rather that it was merely the result of *custom and form*, and that it was done because it was expected to be done, for it was the Church's order after the Lord's supper to kiss one another.

It was on this ground that it seemed to me to be most pernicious; and I could have known how it would work, even though I had not actually been told, that sometimes sisters had stayed away from the Lord's supper, because they did not feel comfortable in kissing all the women in the church.

When therefore I began to break bread with the brethren, I did not kiss one brother after the breaking of bread; but I made a point of it to kiss every one of them on that very day at a later meeting, when I left to go to my lodgings, in order that no one would be able to say it was pride or lack of love in me that I had not kissed them.

Thus I did on the second Lord's day and on the third. On the fourth Lord's day a brother said, after the breaking of bread, 'Brethren, shall we give one another the brotherly kiss.' I was then ready at once, like the rest to kiss all the brethren. But the next time there was no kissing, and thus the *mere cold form* was banished, and every brother felt free to kiss another brother when his heart bade him do so, without being bound to it by custom or form. I have so circumstantially dwelt on these apparently little things, because I think them, in principle, matters of the deepest importance (N1, 1843).

Aiming after life, power and reality

Everything that is a mere form, a mere habit and custom in divine things, is to be dreaded exceedingly: *life, power, reality*, this is what we have to aim after. Things should not result from without, but from within. The sort of clothes I wear, the kind of house I live in, the quality of the furniture I use, all such like things should not result from other persons doing so and so, or because it is customary among those brethren with whom I associate to live in a simple, inexpensive, self-denying way. Whatever be done in these things, in the way of giving up, or self-denial, or deadness to the world, should result from the joy we have in God, and from the entering into the preciousness of our future inheritance.

Far better that for the time being we stand still, and do not take the steps we see others take, than that it is merely the force of example that leads us to do a thing, and afterwards it be regretted. Not that I mean in the least by this to imply we should continue to live in luxury, self-indulgence, and the like, whilst others are in great need. But we should begin the thing in a right way, that is, aim after the right state of heart; begin *inwardly* instead of *outwardly*. If otherwise, it will not last. We shall look back, or even get into a worse state than we were before.

But oh! how different if joy in God leads us to any little act of self-denial. How gladly we do it then! How great an honour then do we count it to be! How much does the heart then long to be able to do more for Him who has done so much for us!

We are far then from looking down in proud self-complacency upon those who do not go as far as we do, but rather pray to the Lord that He would be pleased to help our dear brethren and sisters forward who may seem to us weak in any particular point; and we are also conscious to ourselves that if we have a little more light or strength with reference to one point, other brethren may have more light or grace in other respects (N1, 1843).

Treasures in Heaven . . .

Matthew 6:19–21. 'Do not store up for yourselves treasures on earth, where moth and rust destroy, and where thieves break in and steal. But store up for yourselves treasures in heaven, where moth and rust do not destroy, and where thieves do not break in and steal. For where your treasure is, there your heart will be also.' It is the Lord Jesus, our Lord and Master, who speaks this. He who has infinite wisdom and unfathomable love to us, who therefore both knows what is for our real welfare and happiness. He cannot exact from us any requirement inconsistent with that love which led Him to lay down His life for us.

Remembering who it is who speaks to us in these verses, let us consider them. His counsel, His affectionate entreaty, and His commandment to us His disciples is: 'Do not store up for yourselves treasures on earth'. The meaning obviously is that the disciples of the Lord Jesus, being strangers and pilgrims on earth, that is neither belonging to the earth nor expecting to remain in it, *should not seek to increase their earthly possessions*, in whatever these possessions may consist.

This is a word for poor believers as well as for rich believers; it has as much to do with putting shillings into the savings' bank as to putting thousands of pounds into the funds, or purchasing one house or farm after another (N1, 1844).

. . . Providing for children and old age

It may be said, 'But does not every prudent and provident person seek to increase his means, that he may have a goodly portion to leave to his children, or to have something for old age, or for the time of sickness.'

My reply is, 'It is quite true that this is the custom of the world. It was thus in the days of our Lord, and Paul refers to this custom of the world when he says, "Children should not have to save up for their parents, but parents for their children" (2 Cor. 12:14). But whilst thus it is in the world, and we have every reason to believe ever will be so among

80

hose that are of the world, and who therefore have their portion on earth, we disciples of the Lord Jesus, being born again, being children of God not nominally, but really, being truly partakers of the divine nature, being in fellowship with the Father and the Son, and having in prospect "an inheritance that can never perish, spoil or fade" (1 Pet. 1:4), ought in every respect to act differently from the world, and so in this matter also.'

If we disciples of the Lord Jesus seek, like the people of the world, after an increase of our possessions, may not those who are of the world justly question whether we believe what we say, when we speak about our inheritance, our heavenly calling and our being called the children of God? Often it must be a sad stumbling block to the unbeliever to see a professed believer in the Lord Jesus acting in this particular just like himself (N1, 1844).

. . . An objection answered

I have more than once had the following passage quoted to me as a proof that parents ought to lay up money for their children, or husbands for their wives: 'If anyone does not provide for his relatives, and especially for his immediate family, he has denied the faith and is worse than an unbeliever' (1 Tim. 5:8). It is however concerning this verse only necessary in childlike simplicity to read the connection from verse 3 to 5, and it will be obvious that the meaning is this: that whilst the poor widows of the Church are to be cared for by the Church, yet if any needy believing widow had children or grandchildren (not nephews), these children or grandchildren should provide for the widow, that the Church might not be charged; but that, if a believer's child, or grandchild, in such a case did not do so, such a one did not act according to the obligations laid upon him by his holy faith, and was worse than an unbeliever.

Not a word, then, is there in this passage to favour the laying up of treasures upon earth for our children, or our wives (N1, 1844).

. . . No reality in anything but heavenly things

Our Lord says concerning the earth that it is a place 'where moth and rust destroy, and where thieves break in and steal' (Matt. 6:19). All that is of the earth, and in any way connected with it, is subject to corruption, to change, to dissolution. There is no reality, or substance, in anything but heavenly things. Often the careful amassing of earthly possessions ends in losing them in a moment of fire, by robbery, by a change of mercantile concerns, or by loss of work.

But suppose all this were not the case, still, yet a little while, and your soul shall be required of you; or, yet a little while, and the Lord Jesus will return; and what profit will you then have, dear reader, if you have carefully sought to increase your earthly possessions?

My brother, if there were one particle of real benefit to be derived from it, would not He, whose love to us has been proved to the uttermost, have wished that you and I should have it? If, in the least degree, it could tend to the increase of our peace, or joy in the Holy Spirit, or heavenly-mindedness, He, who laid down His life for us, would have commanded us to 'store up treasure on earth' (N1, 1844).

. . . The bank of Heaven

Our Lord however does not merely bid us *not* to store up treasure on earth. If He had said no more, His commandment might be abused, and persons might find it an encouragement for their extravagant habits, for their love of pleasure, for their habit of spending everything they have, or can obtain, on themselves. It does not mean, then, as is the common phrase, that we should 'live up to our income'; for, He adds: 'But store up for yourselves treasures in heaven' (Matt. 6:20).

There is such a thing as storing up as truly in Heaven as there is storing up on earth; if it were not so our Lord would have said so. Just as persons put one sum after another into the bank, and it is put down to their credit, and they may use the money afterwards – so truly the penny, the shilling, the pound, the hundred pounds, the ten thousand pounds *given for the Lord's sake, and constrained by the love of Jesus,* to poor brethren, or in any way spent in the work of God, He marks down in the book of remembrance, He considers as laid up in Heaven. *The money is not lost, it is laid up in the bank of Heaven;* yet so, that, whilst an earthly bank may break, or through earthly circumstances we may lose our earthly possessions, the money which is thus secured in Heaven *cannot be lost* (N1, 1844).

. . . Being rich towards God

Treasures stored up on earth bring along with them many cares; treasures stored up in Heaven never give care. Treasures stored up on earth never can afford spiritual joy; treasures stored up in Heaven bring along with them peace and joy in the Holy Spirit even now. Treasures stored up on earth, in a dying hour, cannot afford peace and comfort, and when life is over they are taken from us; treasures stored up in Heaven draw forth thanksgiving that we were permitted and counted worthy to serve the Lord with the means with which He was pleased to entrust us as stewards; and when this life is over we are not deprived of what was stored up there, but when we go to Heaven we go to the place where our treasures are, and we shall find them there.

Often we hear it said when a person has died: he died worth so much. But it is certain that a person may die worth fifty thousand pounds, as the world reckons, and yet that individual may not possess, in the sight of God, one thousand pounds, because he *was not rich towards God*, he did not store up treasure in Heaven. And so, on the other hand, we can suppose a man falling asleep in Jesus, and his surviving widow finding scarcely enough left behind to suffice for the funeral, who was nevertheless *rich towards God*; in the sight of God he may possess five thousand pounds – he may have stored that sum in Heaven . . .

Suppose after a little while you should fall asleep, someone may say your wife and child will be unprovided for, because you did not make provision for them. My reply is, 'The Lord will take care of them. The Lord will abundantly provide for them, as He now abundantly provides for us' (N1, 1844).

. . . Strengthening the divine nature

The Lord lastly adds: 'For where your treasure is, there your heart will be also' (Matt. 6:21). Where should the heart of the disciple of the Lord Jesus be, but in Heaven? Our calling is a heavenly calling, our inheritance is a heavenly inheritance, and reserved for us in Heaven; our citizenship is in Heaven; but if we believers in the Lord Jesus store up treasures on earth, the necessary result of it is that our hearts will be upon earth; the very fact of our doing so proves that they are there! Nor will it be otherwise till there is a ceasing to store up treasures upon earth.

The believer who stores up treasures upon earth may, at first, not live openly in sin; he in a measure may yet bring some honour to the Lord in certain things; but the injurious tendencies of this habit will show themselves more and more, whilst the habit of storing up treasures in Heaven

84

would draw the heart more and more heavenward; would be continually strengthening his new, his divine nature, his spiritual faculties, because it would call his spiritual faculties into use, and thus they would be strengthened; and he would more and more, whilst yet in the body, have his heart in Heaven, and set upon heavenly things. Thus the storing up of treasures in Heaven would bring along with it, even in this life, precious spiritual blessings as a reward of obedience to the commandment of our Lord (N1, 1844).

The great business of the disciple of the Lord Jesus

Matthew 6:33 'Seek first his kingdom and his righteousness, and all things will be given to you as well.' The great business which the disciple of the Lord Jesus has to be concerned about (for this word was spoken to disciples, to professed believers) is to seek the Kingdom of God. That is, to seek, as I view it, after the external and internal prosperity of the Church of Christ.

If, according to our ability, and according to the opportunity which the Lord gives us, we seek to win souls for the Lord Jesus, that appears to me to be seeking the *external prosperity* of the Kingdom of God. And if we, as members of the body of Christ, seek to benefit our fellow members in the body, helping them on in grace and truth, or caring for them in any way, that would be seeking the *internal prosperity* of the Kingdom of God.

But in connection with this we have also 'to seek His righteousness', which means, (as it was spoken to disciples, to those who have a Father in Heaven, and not to those who were without), to seek to be more and more like God, to seek to be inwardly conformed to the mind of God.

If these two things are attended to, (and they imply also that we are not slothful in business), then do we come under that precious promise: 'And all these things (that is food, clothing, or anything else we need for this present life) will be given to you as well.' It is not *for* attending to these things that we obtain the blessing, but *in* attending to them.

I now ask you, my dear reader, a few questions in all love, because I do seek your welfare, and I do not wish to put these questions to you, without putting them first to my own heart.

Do you make it your primary business, your first great concern, to seek the Kingdom of God and His righteousness?

Are the things of God, the honour of His name, the welfare of His Church, the conversion of sinners and the profit of your own soul, your chief aim?

Or does your business, or your family, or your own temporal concerns, in some shape or other *primarily* occupy your attention?

Remember that the world passes away, but the things of God endure for ever. I never knew a child of God who acted according to the above passage, in whose experience the Lord did not fulfil His word of promise 'All these things will be given to you as well' (N1, 1844).

Assurance . . .

As there are so many children of God who *do not know* that they are children of God; as there are so many whose sins are forgiven who *do not know* that they are forgiven; and as there are so many who will be saved, who *do not know* that they will be saved, and who are continually afraid of what will become of them, were they to be taken out of the world, I say something here on this most important subject.

Question. How may I obtain the knowledge that I am a child of God, or that I am born again, or that my sins are forgiven, or that I shall not perish but have everlasting life?

86

Answer. Not by feelings, not by a dream, not by my experience being like this or that one's, or unlike this or that one's. This matter is to be settled, as all other spiritual matters, entirely by *the revealed will of God*, the written Word of God, which is the *only* rule, the *only* standard for believers.

Question. By what passages, then, for instance, may I make out that I am a child of God, or born again?

Answer. In 1 John 5:1, it is written: 'Everyone who believes that Jesus is the Christ is born of God.' The meaning of these words is evidently this, that everyone (whether young or old, male or female, one who has lived an outwardly moral or immoral life), who believes that the poor, despised Jesus of Nazareth, was the promised Christ or Messiah, such a one is no longer in his natural state, but is born again, is born of God, is a child of God.

The question therefore is, 'Do you believe in Jesus, who was born at Bethlehem, and crucified under Pontius Pilate, is the promised Saviour, the Messiah, the one for whom the Jews were to look?' If so, you are a child of God, else you would not believe it. It is given unto you to believe it. Millions may *say* that Jesus is the Saviour, the Messiah, but none *believe* it except the children of God. It proves me to be a child of God that I believe it; to none besides is it given to *believe* it, though millions might *say* so (N1, 1845).

. . . Knowledge and enjoyment

Question. But I do not feel that I am born again, born of God, and I have therefore no enjoyment.
Answer. In order that you may have the enjoyment which is

the result of the knowledge that you are a child of God, or born again, you must receive God's testimony. He is a faithful witness. He speaks nothing but the truth. His declaration is that, 'Everyone who believes that Jesus is the Christ is born of God' (1 John 5:1). If you receive this testimony of God, you, to whom by grace it is given to believe that Jesus is the Christ, cannot but be happy from the fact that God Himself says that you are His child.

But if you will wait till you *feel* that you are a child of God, you may have to wait long; and even if you felt it, yet your feelings would be worth nothing: for either it might be a false feeling, or though it were real, it might be lost the next hour. Feelings change, but the Word of God remains unalterably the same.

You have then, without having had a dream about it, without having had a portion of the Word in a more than usual way impressed upon your mind concerning the subject, without having heard something like a voice from Heaven about it, to say to yourself, 'If I believe that Jesus is the promised Messiah, I am a child of God.' And then, *from a belief of what God declares in this passage* concerning you who believe that Jesus is the Christ, even that you are His child, spring peace and joy in the Holy Spirit (N1, 1845).

. . . Knowing I'm forgiven when I don't feel it

Question. How may I know that my sins are forgiven? Have I to wait till I feel that they are forgiven before I take comfort concerning this matter? Or must I wait till I have in some powerful way a portion of the Word of God applied to my mind to assure me of it?

Answer. This point is again only to be settled by the Word of God. We have not to wait till we *feel* that our sins are forgiven. I myself have now been a believer for more than nineteen years (that is, in the year 1845). How long it is since I have had no doubt whatever about the forgiveness of my sins I cannot tell with certainty; but this I am quite sure of, that ever since I have been in England, which is now about sixteen years, I have never once had a single moment's doubt that my sins are all forgiven; yet I do not remember that I even once have *felt* they were forgiven. To *know* they are forgiven, and to *feel* they are forgiven are two different things.

The way to settle whether our sins are forgiven is to refer to the Word of God alone. In Acts 10:43 it is written concerning the Lord Jesus, 'All the prophets testify about him that everyone who believes in him receives forgiveness of sins through his name.'

The questions therefore to be put to ourselves are simply these: 'Do I walk in utter carelessness? Do I trust in my own exertions for salvation? Do I expect forgiveness for my sins on account of living a better life in the future?' Or, 'Do I depend only upon this, that Jesus died upon the cross to save sinners – and that Jesus fulfilled the law of God to make sinners righteous?' If the latter is the case, my sins are forgiven whether I feel it or not (N1, 1845).

. . . Do you confess Jesus as Lord?

Question. How may I know that I shall be saved?
Answer (Romans 10:9). 'If you confess with your mouth, "Jesus is Lord", and believe in your heart that God raised him from the dead, you will be saved.' The point is simply this: 'Do I confess with my mouth the Lord Jesus? Do I own Him by confession of my mouth before men, and do I believe in my heart that Jesus of Nazareth who was

crucified was not left in the grave, but was raised up again by God on the third day?' If so, I shall be saved.

For while there may be the confession of the Lord Jesus with the mouth, without the person being finally saved, there does not go along with this the believing in the heart that God has raised Him from the dead, without the person in whom *both* are found being finally saved. In none but the children of God are these two points found united together. We have here particularly to observe that it is not written: 'If you *say* that God raised Him from the dead', but 'If you *believe in your heart* that God raised Him from the dead, you will be saved.'

I have then to take God at His word. If I confess the Lord Jesus with my mouth, and believe in my heart that God raised Him from the dead, I shall be saved, though I do not *feel* it, though I am utterly unworthy of salvation, though I am altogether deserving condemnation. I must not wait till I *feel* that I shall be saved before I take comfort. But I must believe what God says in this verse, and out of *that*, peace and comfort will flow to my soul.

Should however one or other of the children of God believe in his heart the resurrection of the Lord Jesus, if at the same time he has never confessed with his mouth, he cannot be surprised that the assurance about his salvation is lacking in him. But if both are found in you, dear reader, God has been gracious to you, you are His child, you will be saved (N1, 1845).

. . . How may I know that I am a chosen one?

Question. How may I know that I am one of the elect? I often read in the Scriptures about election, and I often hear about election, how may I know that I am a chosen one, that I am predestined to be conformed to the image of the Son of God?

Answer. Acts 13:48. 'All who were appointed for eternal life believed.' The question therefore simply is this: 'Do I believe in the Lord Jesus? Do I take Him to be the one whom God declares Him to be, that is, His beloved Son in whom He is well pleased?' If so, I am a believer, and I should never have believed except I had been appointed by God to eternal life – except I had been made by God to be a vessel of mercy. Therefore the matter is a very simple one: if I believe in the Lord Jesus I am a chosen one, I have been appointed to eternal life.

Again, in Romans 8:29–30, it is written: 'For those God foreknew he also predestined to be conformed to the likeness of his Son, that he might be the firstborn among many brothers. And those he predestined he also called; those he called, he also justified; those he justified, he also glorified.' How are we justified, or constituted just ones, before God? By faith in the Lord Jesus (Rom. 3:20–6).

Therefore if I believe in the Lord Jesus, it follows (on account of the inseparable connection of all the precious things spoken of in Romans 8:28–9) that I have been foreknown by God, that I have been predestined by Him to be conformed to the image of His Son, that I have been called, that I have been justified, and that, in the sight of God, I am already as good as glorified, though I am not as yet in the actual possession and enjoyment of the glory (N1, 1845).

. . . Why you may lack assurance

The reason why people who renounce confidence in their own goodness for salvation, and who only trust in the merits and sufferings of the Lord Jesus, do not know that they are the children of God, that their sins are forgiven, and that they are saved, generally arises from one of these things:

1. They do not know the simplicity of the Gospel; or

2. They seek to settle it by their feelings; or

3. They wait for some powerful impulse, or a dream, or something like a voice from Heaven to assure them of it, or for some passage being in a powerful way applied to their mind to assure them of it; or

4. Because they are living in sin.

Should the last be the case, then, however correctly we may understand the Gospel; however much we may desire by the Holy Scriptures alone to settle these questions; however much in former times we may have enjoyed the assurance of the forgiveness of our sins, or of our being the children of God, or that we shall be saved: in such a state of heart all peace would be gone, and would not return as long as we live in sin.

There may be found much weakness and many infirmities even in the believer who has assurance about these points; but the Holy Spirit does not comfort us and will not comfort us, if we habitually indulge in those things which we know to be contrary to the mind of God. An upright honest heart is of the upmost importance in all divine things; and especially with reference to the assurance about our standing before God (N1, 1845).

A most lovely and gracious clergyman

In Germany –

We then travelled either in the Rhine steamers, or on the rail-road, or in an omnibus, the four following days also, yet so that we arranged to have time to ourselves, and reached Stuttgart about eight o'clock on the Monday evening, July 28.

Of the journey I would mention no more than that on the last day we travelled with a most lovely and gracious brother, an English clergyman from Sussex, with whom, after two or three hours I was so one in heart, that on getting out of the omnibus, in which we travelled together about 30 miles, in order to walk up a long hill, we walked together arm in arm.

It was most refreshing to our spirits to find so lovely a brother in this dark land. We spent a few hours together in Stuttgart, and then this dear brother left for the neighbourhood of Munich, the capital of the kingdom of Bavaria, where his family is for a season (N1, 1845).

'I cast myself flat down upon my face'

July 6, 1846. The reason why, for several months, there had come in so little for the building fund, appeared to me this, that we did not need the money at present; and that, when it was needed, and when my faith and patience had been sufficiently tried, the Lord would send more means. And thus it has proved; for today was given to me the sum of two thousand and fifty pounds, of which two thousand pounds is for the building fund, and fifty pounds for present necessities, of which latter sum I took one half for the present use of the orphans, and the other half for the school, Bible, tract, and missionary fund.

This is the largest donation I have yet had at one time for the work; but I expect still larger ones, in order that more and more it may be manifest to the children of God that there is no *happier*, no *easier*, and no *better* way for obtaining money or anything else in the work of God, than to deal directly with God Himself.

It is impossible to describe my joy in God when I received this donation. I was neither excited nor surprised; for I *look out* for answers to my prayers. I *believe that God hears me*. Yet my heart was so full of joy that I could only sit before God, and admire Him, like David in 2 Samuel 7. At last I cast myself flat down upon my face, and burst forth in thanksgiving to God, and in surrendering my heart afresh to Him for His blessed service (J, 1846).

After eleven hundred and ninety-five days prayer . . .

February 12, 1849. The new orphan house is now almost entirely finished. In six weeks, with the help of God, all will be completed. On this account I have been during the last fortnight much occupied in making the necessary arrangements for fitting it up and furnishing it; but the more I have been occupied with this the more I have seen how large a sum the whole of the fittings and the furniture will require; and this consideration has led me still more earnestly of late to entreat the Lord that He would be pleased to give me the means which may yet be needed for the completion of the whole.

Under these circumstances a brother in the Lord came to me this morning, and after a few minutes' conversation gave me two thousand pounds, concerning which sum he kindly gave me permission to use it for the fitting up and furnishing of the new orphan house, or for anything else needed in connection with the orphans. I have placed the whole of this sum, at least for the present, to the building fund.

Now, dear reader, place yourself in my position. Eleven hundred and ninety-five days it is since I began asking the Lord for means for the building and fitting up of an orphan house. Day by day have I, by His grace, since that time, continued to bring this matter before Him. Without one moment's doubt, or misgiving, or wavering, have I been enabled to trust in God for the means. From the beginning, after I had once ascertained the will of God concerning this work, have I been assured that He would bring it about. As sure have I been from the beginning that He would do so, as if I had already had all the means in hand for it, or as if the house had been actually before me occupied by children.

But though to faith even three years ago the whole work was accomplished, to sight there remained many and great difficulties in the way of means, as well as in other respects. Therefore I was on the point of giving myself again especially to prayer at the very moment when I was informed that the donor of the above mentioned two thousand pounds had called to see me (J, 1849).

... inexpressible delight in God

February 12, 1849 (cont.). Now I have the means, as far as I can see, which will enable me to meet all the expenses; and in all probability I shall have even several hundred pounds more than are needed. Thus the Lord shows that He can and will not only give as *much as is absolutely needed* for His work, but also that He can and will give *abundantly*.

It is impossible to describe the real joy I had in God when I received this sum. I was calm, not in the least excited, able to go on immediately with other work that came upon me at once after I had received the donation; but inexpressible was the delight which I had in God, who had thus given me the full answer to my thousands of prayers, during these eleven hundred and ninety-five days.

I notice further concerning this donation:

1. The donor especially desired to keep his name entirely concealed; and in order that no one might know who he is,

he gave me not an order on a bank, but brought the amount in notes.

2. He had intended to leave me this sum for the benefit of the orphans after his death, and for years it had been in his last will; but he judged it more according to the will of God to give it during his lifetime (J, 1849).

Numberless ways in which God helps

January 9, 1850. Today was sent to me from the Committee of the Cholera Fund in Bristol twenty pounds. The gentlemen constituting the fund had voted for the benefit of the twenty children who had lost their parents in the cholera, and whom I had received into the New Orphan House.

I had not applied either directly or indirectly for this money; indeed I was reluctant even to give information as to the number of cholera orphans received, lest there should be even the appearance that after all I asked for money, instead of solely trusting in the living God. But some of the gentlemen on the committee, knowing the fact that I had received many orphans, made such by means of the cholera, proposed that there should be paid to the institution a sovereign on account of each such child received. The sum was especially remarkable to me as a fresh proof of the numberless ways which God has at His command for providing me with means.

I also cannot help noticing the remarkable coincidence that, at the time God visited this land with cholera in 1849, I had so much room for the reception of orphans. The Lord was pleased to allow me the joy and sweet privilege of receiving altogether twenty-six children from ten months old upward, who lost their parents from cholera *at that time*, and many besides since then, who were bereaved of their parents through this fearful malady (J, 1850).

Keeping poor orphans from prison

The moral state of the poorhouses greatly influences me to go forward. I have heard it again and again, from good authority, that children placed in the Unions are corrupted, on account of the children of vagrants and other very bad young people who are in such places. So many poor relatives of orphans, though unable to provide for them, cannot bear the idea of their going there, lest they should be corrupted.

I therefore judge that, even for the sake of keeping orphans of poor but respectable people from being obliged to mix with the children of vagabonds, I ought to do, to my utmost power, all I can to help them. For this reason, then, I purpose, in dependence upon the living God, to go forward and to establish another orphan house for seven hundred destitute children, who are bereaved of both parents. [Müller actually built two further orphan houses to care for this number of children.] When writing thus about the poorhouses, I do not wish to be understood in the way of reproof, for I know not how these matters could be altered – but simply to state the fact that thus it is.

In this purpose I am the more confirmed, since it is a fact that the orphan houses already in existence in the kingdom are by no means sufficient to admit *even the most deserving and distressing cases*, and far less all that it would be well to provide for. Moreover there is great difficulty connected with the admission of orphans into most of the ordinary orphan establishments, on account of the votes which must be obtained, so that *really* needy persons have neither time nor money to obtain them. Does not the fact that there were six thousand young orphans in the prisons of England about five years ago call aloud for an extension of orphan institutions? By God's help, I will do what I can to keep poor orphans from prison (N2, 1851).

A voice from Heaven

January 4, 1851. Besides donations from Newton Ferrers, Keswick, and Bath, I received also this morning anonymously from Torquay five shillings worth of postage stamps with these words: 'Open thy mouth wide, and I will fill it.' I am doing this. I expect much, very much indeed, in every way. I also expect much in the way of means.

Evening. This very day the Lord has given me a most precious proof that He delights in our having large expectations from Him. 'My mouth has been filled' according to the portion of Holy Scripture sent to me this morning. I have received this evening the sum of three thousand pounds, being the largest donation I have ever had as yet. I now write again that I expect far larger sums still, in order that it may be yet more manifest that there is no happier, no easier, and no better way of obtaining pecuniary means for the work of the Lord than the one in which I have been led.

How great my joy in God is, on account of this donation, cannot be described; but it is not in the least coupled with excitement. I take this donation out of the hands of the living God. I continually look for His help, and am perfectly assured that I shall have it, and therefore my soul is calm and peaceful, without any excitement, though the donation is so large.

This donation is however like a voice from Heaven, speaking to me concerning a most deeply important matter respecting which I am seeking guidance from the Lord, the building of another orphan house. For several years while the orphans were living in rented houses in Wilson Street, Bristol, it pleased the Lord to manifest His power by helping us from day to day, and sometimes even from meal to meal. But in recent years He has been pleased to show us His power by sending us abundant supplies (J, 1851).

A kind of secret joy

The greatness of the sum required [to build two further orphan houses on Ashley Down], affords me a kind of secret joy; for the greater the difficulty to be overcome, the more will it be seen to the glory of God how much can be done by prayer and faith; and also, because, when God Himself overcomes our difficulties for us, we have, in this very fact, the assurance that we are engaged in His work and not in our own (N2, 1851).

The joy which such answers to prayer give cannot be described [he had just received a donation of over five thousand pounds]; and the impetus which they thus afford to the spiritual life is exceedingly great. The experience of this happiness I desire for all my Christian readers. Nor is there anything to hinder any believer from having these joys. If you believe indeed in the Lord Jesus for the salvation of your soul, if you walk uprightly and do not regard iniquity in your heart, if you continue to wait patiently and believingly upon God – then answers will surely be given to your prayers.

You may not be called upon to serve the Lord in the way the writer does, and therefore may never have answers to prayer respecting such things as are recorded here; but in your various circumstances as to your family, your business, your profession, your church position, your labour for the Lord, you may have answers as distinct as any here recorded (N2, 1854).

The secret of success

The disciples of the Lord Jesus should labour with all their might in the work of God, as if everything depended upon their own exertions. And yet, having done so, they should not in the least trust in their labour and efforts, and in the means which they use for the spread of the truth, but in God. They should with all earnestness seek the blessing of God in persevering, patient, and believing prayer.

Here is the great secret of success. Work with all your might; but trust not in the least in your work. Pray with all your might for the blessing of God; but work, at the same time, with all diligence, with all patience, with all perseverance. Pray then, and work. Work and pray. And still again pray, and then work. And so on all the days of your life. The result will surely be abundant blessing. Whether you see much fruit or little fruit; such kind of service will be blessed (N2, 1853).

Tears of joy

June 13, 1853. We were now very poor. Not indeed in debt, nor was even all the money gone; for there was still about twelve pounds in hand; but then there needed to be bought flour, of which we buy generally ten sacks at a time, three hundred stones of oatmeal, four hundred-weight of soap, and there were many little repairs going on the house, with a number of workmen, besides the regular current expenses of about seventy pounds per week. Over and above all this, on Saturday, the day before yesterday, I found that the heating apparatus needed to be repaired, which would cost in all probability twenty-five pounds.

It was therefore desirable, humanly speaking, to have a hundred pounds for these heavy extra expenses, besides means for the current expenses. But I had no human prospect of getting even a hundred pence, much less a hundred pounds. In addition to this, today was Monday, when generally the income is little. But in walking to the orphan house this morning, and praying as I went, I particularly told the Lord in prayer that on this day, though Monday, He could send much. And thus it was.

I received this morning three hundred and one pounds for the Lord's service, as might be most needed. The joy which I had cannot be described. I walked up and down in my room for a long time, tears of joy and gratitude to the Lord running plentifully over my cheeks, praising and magnifying the Lord for His goodness, and surrendering myself afresh with all my heart to Him for His blessed service. I scarcely ever felt more the kindness of the Lord in helping me (J, 1853).

A specific prayer answered

May 23, 1854. Yesterday I looked over the list of the 56 labourers in the Word [home and foreign missionaries], whom I seek to assist, in order to see to whom it would be desirable to send help. Having drawn out a list, with the respective amounts for each, I found that it would be desirable to send out this week three hundred and twenty-seven pounds, but I wanted at least fifty pounds more to be able to accomplish this.

Accordingly I gave myself to prayer that it might please the Lord to send me the means. And now this morning, in answer to prayer, I received anonymously from bankers in London one hundred pounds, which the donor desired to be applied for the current expenses for the orphans, and for labourers in the Gospel at home and abroad. I took therefore fifty pounds for the orphans, and fifty pounds for home and foreign labourers.

By the same post I received also from the neighbourhood of Shrewsbury ten pounds, the disposal of which being left to me, I took for missionary objects.

I have now the desire of my heart granted – being able to send out the full amount of what it yesterday appeared to me desirable that I should send to the brethren whom I seek to help (J, 1854).

Following a poor young sinner with prayer

We were obliged to expel one boy from the establishment. This boy was admitted on October 4, 1849. He was then not quite eight years old; but though so young, it was soon found out that he was old in sin, for he was a confirmed liar and thief. He gloried in it among the other boys, and told them that he belonged to a juvenile gang of thieves, before he had been admitted into the orphan house, that he had stolen from the ships iron, brass and other metals, and sold it.

We thought at first that he spoke thus merely in the way of boasting, but it proved but too true and that he was experienced in such matters. Twice he ran away from the orphan house, carrying off things belonging to the other children. Moreover he could pick locks. We received him back twice, after having run away, hoping that, by bearing with him, admonishing him, speaking to him privately, praying with him, and using a variety of other means, he might be reclaimed; but all in vain.

At last, having borne with him, and tried him for five years and four months, he was solemnly, with prayer, before the whole establishment, expelled, if by any means this last painful remedy might be blessed to him.

Yet we follow even this poor young sinner with our prayers, and hope that yet the Lord might show him his evil ways, and give us even now joy concerning him, as we have had before in a similar instance. This case afresh deeply impressed upon me the importance of caring for orphans from their earliest days; for this poor young boy, when but eight years old, was already greatly practised in stealing (N2, 1855).

How to trust God for your personal income

If any one desires to go this way, he must:

1. Not *merely say* that he trusts God but *really do so*. Often individuals profess to trust God, but they embrace every opportunity, directly or indirectly, to expose their need, and thus seek to induce people to help them. I do not say it is wrong to make known our wants; but I do say it ill agrees with trust in God to expose our wants for the sake of inducing persons to help us. God will take us at our word. If we say that we trust Him, He will try whether we *really* do so, or only profess to do so; and if *indeed* we trust Him, we are satisfied to stand with Him alone.

2. The individual who desires to go this way must be willing to be rich or poor, as the Lord pleases. He must be willing to know what it is to have an abundance or scarcely anything. He must be willing to leave this world without any possessions.

3. He must be willing to take the money in God's way, not merely in large sums but in small. Again and again have I had a single shilling given or sent me. To have refused such tokens of Christian love would have been ungracious.

4. He must be willing to live as the Lord's steward. If anyone were to begin this way of living, and did not distribute out of that which the Lord gives to him, but hoard it up – or if he would live up to his income, as it is called – then the Lord, who influences the hearts of His children to help him with means, would soon cause those channels to be dried up (N2, 1855).

For twenty-five years . . .

It is now above twenty-five years since I have had any regular income whatever. In the year 1830 I saw it to be the Lord's will to give up my regular income in connection with the ministry of the Word, and to trust in Him alone for the supply of all my temporal necessities. I have been enabled to continue in this path, and have not been allowed to regret the step which I then took.

Thus it is also in my position as director of the various objects of the Scriptural Knowledge Institution. I have no salary in this position, but the Lord abundantly supplies my need; though there are many expenses connected with this position, He abundantly meets all my wants, and gives me far more than I need.

If I had sought to obtain a lucrative place, either as a preacher of the Gospel, or in some other way, I should not have had more, I have reason to believe, if as much, as, unsought, unasked for, so far as it regards man, I receive day by day out of the loving hand of my heavenly Father.

When I look at His kindness to me in saving my guilty soul, I am overwhelmed with the boundlessness of His love and grace towards me in Christ Jesus. When I look at His kindness to me, even as it regards material things, I know not where to begin, nor where to end, in speaking well of His name (N2, 1856).

. . . God has been my helper

I do desire to magnify Him, and therefore declare in this public way His great goodness to me in thus so abundantly supplying my material needs. I do so also, if it may please God, by this means to encourage the hearts of His children more and more unreservedly to trust in Him.

It is now above twenty-five years since I have asked help for myself from any human being; but God has been indeed my helper. And now the very work even with which I am connected, respecting which I had every reason to believe, when I commenced it, that it would be connected with great expenses to myself, as well as to be the means, *looked at naturally*, of decreasing my own income, God has, though unsought for on my part, used as the instrument to bring along with it many supplies for myself also, thus not only abundantly meeting my increased expenses, but giving me far more than I need for myself.

How great is His goodness! Dear Christian reader, be encouraged by this! Do but trust in God with all your heart, and you will find that you will not be confounded. Only let it be trust *in God*, not *in man*, not *in circumstances*, not *in any of your own exertions*, but real trust in God, and you will be helped, in your various needs (N2, 1856).

Unbelief put to shame

Not only does this work continue to exist after more than 22 years, carried on solely through the power of faith in the living God; but also year by year its operations have been extended. Unbelief is thus put to shame. It is plainly proved that the work of God can be carried on simply by trust in God.

If *our work* is indeed *the work of God*, faith and prayer will be found efficient agents; and if they are *not* efficient, we may well question whether we do *indeed* make use of them; or, if we do, whether the work in which we are occupied is *truly* the work of God.

Behold, dear reader, how effectual this way is for obtaining means. Behold too how pleasant a way it is; for I have not to encounter unpleasant refusals in applying for money. Behold how cheap a way; for it involves none of the heavy expenses usually attendant on the collection of contributions. All I do is to make known the work in which we are engaged by means of the reports, which are for the most part sold for the benefit of the orphans, and they actually brought in during this year, as the audited accounts show, a little more than they cost (N2, 1856).

His secret treasure

But perhaps you say, 'Yes, it is just these [Annual] Reports. There is nothing at all remarkable in the matter.'

Our reply is: 'We do not pretend to miracles. We have no desire even that the work in which we are engaged should be considered an extraordinary one, or even a remarkable one. We are truly sorry that many persons inconsiderately look upon it almost as a miraculous one. The principles on which we are acting are as old as the Holy Scriptures. But they are forgotten by many, not held in living faith by others, and by some are not known at all. By not a few, they are denied even to be scriptural, and are considered as wild and fanatical.'

It is ascribed to my being a *foreigner* that I succeed so well; or to the *novelty* of the thing; or to some *secret treasure* to which I have access. But when all will not account for the progress of the work, it is said the reports produce it all.

My reply to these different objections is: 'My being a *foreigner*, looked at naturally, would be more likely to hinder my being entrusted with large sums than to induce donors to give. As to the *novelty* procuring the money, the time is long gone by for novelty, for this is June 1856, and the work commenced in March 1834.

'As to the *secret treasure* to which I have access, there is more in this supposition than the objectors are aware of;

for surely God's treasury is inexhaustible, and I have *that* (though that alone) to go to, and have indeed drawn out of it, simply by prayer and faith, more than one hundred and thirteen thousand pounds since the beginning of the work' (N2, 1856).

God working for us

But now as to the last objection, that the *Reports* are the means by which all the money is obtained. Let us consider this a little for I do heartily desire that you should not lose the blessing which this institution is intended to convey to your soul.

My reply is: 'There is nothing unusual in writing reports. This is done by public institutions generally, but the constant complaint is that reports are not read. Our reports are not extraordinary as to the power of language, or as to striking appeals to feelings. They are simple statements of facts. These reports are not accompanied by personal application for means; they are simply sent to the donors, or to any other individuals who wish to have or purchase them. If they produce results, which reports generally do not, I can only ascribe it to the Lord.

'I do not mean to say that God does not use the reports as instruments in procuring us means. They are written in order that I may thus give an account of my stewardship, but particularly in order that, by these printed accounts of the work, the chief end of this institution may be answered, which is to raise another public testimony to an unbelieving world that in these last days the living God is still the living God, listening to the prayers of His children, and helping those who put their trust in Him. I am also anxious that believers generally may be benefited and be encouraged to trust in God for everything they may need, and be stirred up to deal in greater simplicity with God respecting everything connected with their own particular position and circumstances.

'But while these are the *primary* reasons for publishing these reports, we doubt not that the Lord has again and again used them as instruments in leading persons to help us with their means' (N2, 1856).

The opposite to rashness or enthusiasm

Commenting on the receipt of two thousand seven hundred pounds to be used both for his building plans and for missionary work, Müller recorded –

How precious it is to trust in God, *really* to trust in Him! Only try this way and you will know the sweetness and blessedness of it for yourself. But there must be more than merely *saying* I trust in God. Your heart must really look to Him alone. If you do so, then contrary to all natural prospects, you will find how able and how willing He is to help you.

I had no natural prospect of being able to accomplish as much, especially as regards missionary operations, as before. Natural prospects were all against it; yet God, the rich almighty God, whose resources never fail, who is always the living God, the same faithful and unchangeable God, was able to help me. In Him I desire to make my boast.

So fully is my heart assured of His ability and willingness to help me, that by His grace, no amount of need, difficulties, or natural improbabilities, would discourage me, if only I could see that He would have me to act, and that my acting would be for His honour and glory.

To such a conclusion, however, I desire to come most slowly, most patiently, most prayerfully, and only upon

scriptural ground. In this way I desire grace to proceed.
The very opposite to rashness or enthusiasm is what I desire
to aim after (N3, 1859).

The Spirit's guidance and peace

The child who has again and again besought His heavenly
Father not to allow him to be deluded, nor even to make a
mistake, is at peace, perfectly at peace, concerning this
decision [to build the final two orphan houses on Ashley
Down for two thousand children]. He has the assurance
that the decision come to, after much prayer during weeks
and months, is the leading of the Holy Spirit. He therefore
purposes to go forward, assuredly believing that he will not
be confounded, for he trusts in God.

Many and great will be the difficulties. Thousands and
tens of thousands of prayers may have to ascend to God
before the full answer may be obtained. Much exercise of
faith and patience may be required. But in the end it will
again be seen that his servant, who trusts in Him, has not
been confounded (N3, 1861).

When the wells ran dry . . .

*The summer of 1864 was hot and dry: water was scarce in
nearly every county of England. Müller recorded in his
Narratives –*

Long before we felt any want in the orphan houses on
Ashley Down, many thousands of the inhabitants of Bristol
and elsewhere had been tried by the lack of rain. At last

however all our fifteen large cisterns in the new orphan houses one, two and three were empty, and almost all our nine wells in these three houses, most of which are deep, failed also. Even one with a good spring, which never had been out before, was also pumped dry.

Now, dear reader, place yourself in our position. For all the various purposes of these three houses we use from 2,000 to 3,000 gallons of water daily. Under these circumstances we were daily waiting upon God, that He would be pleased to give us rain to supply our cisterns and wells, or that He would otherwise help us. Now see how kindly He answered.

About one third of a mile from the orphan houses lives a farmer, who had three wells, filled with water, which he had never known to fail. He very kindly sent word to say that he would gladly supply the orphan houses with water as long as he had any. This was thankfully accepted as a precious answer to prayer, and we had the water hauled, about 1,000 or 1,500 gallons daily. The remainder of what we required was supplied by what our wells yielded, by being pumped every four or six hours. Thus we went on, day by day, and were helped over a most difficult time, whilst the distress in Bristol increased more and more (N3, 1865).

. . . our hope was in God

At last, however, these wells, which never had failed before, and out of which, day by day, for about six weeks, we had drawn so much, without the least apparent diminution at first, were nearly emptied. The kind farmer was under the necessity, though reluctantly, of letting me know that he would need the little water that remained for himself and his tenants.

We thanked God for having helped us for about six weeks in the way mentioned, and asked Him for further help, though we knew not how help was to come. The scarcity of water was now all around greater than ever. Our hope however was in God, being fully assured that this time also we should prove His faithfulness.

On the very day on which the information was received that that day would be the last day we could be supplied with water from those wells, another kind farmer, about a mile and a half from the orphan houses sent word to me that we could have as much water as we liked from a brook which ran through his fields. This offer was kindly accepted. We made a dam in his brook which soon made the water rise to four feet high. Thus we had an abundance of water till God was pleased to send rain. The only difference in the latter case was that we needed three carts, instead of one or two, and several men more than before. Thus by prayer we were helped through the great drought of the summer of 1864 (N3, 1864).

The most important business of your life

From a New Year's address –

We have through the Lord's goodness been permitted to enter upon another year. The minds of many of us will no doubt be occupied with plans for the future, and the various spheres of service in which we shall be engaged. The welfare of our families, the prosperity of our business, our work and service for the Lord, may be considered the most important matters to be attended to. But, according to my judgment, the most important point to be attended to is this: *Above all things, see to it that your souls are happy in the Lord.*

Other things may press upon you. The Lord's work ever may have urgent claims upon your attention. But I deliberately repeat, it is of supreme and paramount importance that you should seek to have your souls truly happy in God Himself. Day by day seek to make this the most important business of your life. This has been my firm and settled conviction for the last thirty-five years.

For the first four years after my conversion I knew not its vast importance. But now, after much experience, I specially commend this point to the notice of my younger brethren and sisters in Christ. The secret of all true effectual service is – joy in God, and having experimental acquaintance and fellowship with God Himself (U, 1864).

The secret of happiness

But in what way shall we attain to this settled happiness of soul? How shall we learn to enjoy God? How shall we obtain such an all-sufficient soul-satisfying portion in Him as shall enable us to let go the things of this world as vain and worthless in comparison?

I answer: 'This happiness is to be obtained through the study of the Holy Scriptures. God has therein revealed Himself unto us in the face of Jesus Christ.'

In the Scriptures, by the power of the Holy Spirit, He makes Himself known unto our souls. Remember it is not a god of our own thoughts or our own imaginations that we need to be acquainted with, but the God of the Bible, our Father, who has given the blessed Jesus to die for us. Him should we seek intimately to know, according to the revelation He has made of Himself in His own most precious Word . . . (U, 1864).

The God of Elijah is here today, and He is exactly the same as He was in the prophet's time – as ready and as willing to help His children. The living God is with us, Whose power never fails, Whose arm never grows weary, Whose wisdom is infinite, and Whose power is unchanging.

Therefore today, tomorrow, and next month, as long as life is continued, He will be our helper and friend. Still more, even as he is through all time, so will He be through all eternity (W, undated).

'The Lord's actings upon me'

July 25, 1865. From the neighbourhood of London, one hundred pounds with the following letter –
'My dear Sir, I believe that it is through the Lord's acting upon me that I enclose you a cheque on the Bank of England, Western Branch, for one hundred pounds. I hope that your affairs are going on well. Yours in the Lord, ———.'

This Christian gentleman, whom I have never seen, and who is engaged in a very large business in London, had sent me several times before a similar sum. A day or two before I received this last kind donation, I had asked the Lord that He would be pleased to influence the heart of this donor to help me again. I had never done this before regarding him. Thus I had the double answer to prayer, in that not only money came in, but money from *him*.

You will now see the meaning in the donor's letter when he wrote, 'I believe that it is through the Lord's acting upon me that, etc.' It was the Lord who acted upon this gentleman to send me this sum.

Perhaps you may think that in acknowledging the receipt of the donation, I told the donor what I have here stated. I did not. My reason for not doing so was lest he should have thought I was in especial need and might have been thus influenced to send more. In truly knowing the Lord, in

113

really relying upon Him, there is no need of giving hints directly or indirectly, whereby individuals may be induced further to help. I might have written to the donor (as was indeed the case), 'I need a considerable sum day by day for the current expenses of the various objects of the institution', and also might have told him, at that time, that I needed yet about twenty thousand pounds to enable me to meet all the expenses connected with the contemplated enlargement of the orphan work. But my practice is never to allude to any of these things in my correspondence with donors (J, 1865).

The only bond of union

We should not be satisfied unless we come to this state of heart, that we know nothing less among the disciples than that the precious blood of Christ has made us clean. That is the bond of union – that belonging to Christ. One with Christ – that is the great bond to keep before us. The more we realise that the grace of God has apprehended us in Christ, and revealed to our hearts the Lord Jesus Christ, that we are all bought with the same precious blood, that we are all in the same Spirit, that the same life of the risen Jesus is in us, that we are all heirs of God and joint-heirs with Christ, and shall before long enter into the glory of God – if these things were more present to our hearts, how loving, kind, and forbearing would the children of God be!

And yet once more in this nineteenth century it would be said, 'See how these Christians love one another.'

Only let us seek to aim after this, that we see Christ in each other, and not the old nature; the life of the risen Jesus in each other. If we seek to discern Christ in each other, how we shall be drawn to each other! (E, 1866).

114

When mistakes were made

Be slow to take new steps in the Lord's service, or in your own business or in your families. Weigh everything well; weigh all in the light of the Holy Scriptures, and in the fear of God.

Seek to have no will of your own, in order to ascertain the mind of God regarding any steps you propose to take, so that you can honestly say you are willing to do the will of God, if He will only please to instruct you.

But when you have found out what the will of God is, seek for His help, and seek it earnestly, perseveringly, patiently, believingly, and expectingly; and you will surely, in His own time and way, obtain it (N3, 1868).

I never remember, in all my Christian course, a period now of sixty-nine years and four months, that I ever *sincerely* and *patiently* sought to know the will of God by *the teaching of the Holy Spirit*, through the instrumentality of the Word of God, but I have been *always* directed rightly. But if *honesty of heart* and *uprightness before God* were lacking, or if I did not *patiently* wait upon God for my instruction, or if I preferred *the counsel of my fellow-men*, to the declarations of *the Word of the living God*, I made great mistakes (G, 1895).

How to prepare for preaching

I now consider the best mode of preparation for the public ministry of the Word is as follows.

I do not presume to know myself what is best for the hearers, and I therefore ask the Lord in the first place that He would graciously be pleased to teach me on what subject I shall speak, or what portion of His Word I shall expound. Now sometimes it happens that, previous to my asking Him, a subject or passage has been in my mind on which it has appeared well for me to speak. In that case I ask the Lord whether I should speak on this subject or passage. If, after prayer, I feel persuaded that I should, I fix upon it, yet so that I would desire to leave myself open to the Lord to change it if He pleases.

Frequently, however, it occurs that I have no text or subject in my mind before I give myself to prayer for the sake of ascertaining the Lord's will concerning it. In this case I wait some time on my knees for an answer, trying to listen to the voice of the Spirit to direct me. If then a passage or subject, whilst I am on my knees, or after I have finished praying for a text, is brought to my mind, I again ask the Lord, and that sometimes repeatedly, especially if the subject or text should be a peculiar one, whether it be His will that I should speak on such a subject or passage.

If after prayer my mind is peaceful about it, I take this to be the text, but still desire to leave myself open to the Lord for direction, should He please to alter it, or should I have been mistaken (N1, 1869).

How to choose the right text

Frequently it happens that I not only have no text or subject on my mind previous to praying for guidance on this matter, but also I do not obtain one after once, or twice, or more times praying about it. I used formerly at times to be much perplexed when this was the case, but for more than thirty years it has pleased the Lord, in general at least, to keep me in peace about it. What I do is to go on with my regular reading of the Scriptures, where I left off the last time, praying (whilst I read) for a text, now and then also laying aside my Bible for prayer, till I get one.

Thus it has happened that I have read five, ten, yes twenty chapters, before it has pleased the Lord to give me a text. Many times I have even had to go to the place of meeting without one, and obtained it perhaps only a few minutes before I was going to speak. But I have never lacked the Lord's assistance at the time of preaching, provided I had earnestly sought it in private.

The preacher cannot know the particular state of the various individuals who compose the congregation, nor what they require, but the Lord knows it; and if the preacher renounces his own wisdom, he will be assisted by the Lord. If he will choose in his own wisdom, let him not be surprised if he should see little benefit result from his labours (N1, 1869).

After the text is chosen

Now when the text has been obtained, whether it be one or two verses, or a whole chapter or more, I ask the Lord that He would graciously be pleased to teach me by His Holy Spirit whilst meditating over the passage. Within the last thirty-eight years, I have found it the most profitable plan to meditate with my pen in my hand, writing down the outlines as the Word is opened to me. This I do not for the sake of committing them to memory, nor as if I meant to say nothing else, but for the sake of clarity, as being a help to see how much I understand the passage. I also find it useful afterwards to refer to what I have written.

I very seldom use any other help besides that which I understand of the original languages, and some good translations in other languages. My chief help is prayer. I have *never* in my life begun to study one single part of divine truth, without gaining some light about it, when I have been able really to give myself to prayer and meditation over it. But *that* I have often found a difficult matter, partly on account of the weakness of the flesh, and partly also on account of bodily infirmities and multiplicity of engagements.

This I most firmly believe, that no one ought to expect to see much good resulting from his labours in Word and doctrine, if he is not much given to prayer and meditation (N1, 1869).

An even more excellent way

Having prayed and meditated on the subject or text, I desire to leave myself entirely in the hands of the Lord. I ask Him to bring to my mind what I have seen in my room, concerning the subject I am going to speak on, which He generally most kindly does, and often teaches me much additionally while I am preaching.

I must however state that it appears to me there is a preparation for the public ministry of the Word, which is even more excellent than the one I have spoken of. It is this: to live in such *constant* and *real* communion with the Lord, and to be so *habitually* and *frequently* in meditation over the truth, that without the above effort, so to speak, we have obtained food for others, and know the mind of the Lord as to the subject on which we should speak. But this I have only in a small measure experienced, though I desire to be brought into such a state, that habitually 'streams of living water may flow from within me' (John 7:38).

That which I have found most beneficial in my experience for the last thirty-nine years in the public ministry of the Word is *expounding* the Scriptures, and especially the going now and then through a whole gospel or epistle. This may be done in a two-fold way, either by entering minutely into the bearing of every point occurring in the portion, or by giving the general outlines, and thus leading the hearers to see the meaning and connection of the whole (N1, 1869).

The benefits of expository preaching

The benefits which I have seen from *expounding* the Scriptures are these:

1. The hearers are thus, with God's blessing, led to the Scriptures. They find, as it were, a *practical* use of them in the public meetings. This induces them to bring their Bibles, and I have observed that those who at first did not bring them, have afterwards been induced to do so: so that in a short time few of the believers were in the habit of coming without them. This is no small matter; for everything which in our day will lead believers to value the Scriptures is of importance.

2. The expounding of the Scriptures is in general more beneficial to the hearers than if, on a single verse, or half a verse, some remarks are made, so that the portion of Scripture is scarcely anything but a motto for the subject: for few have grace to meditate much over the Word, and thus exposition may not merely be the means of opening up to them the Scriptures, but may create in them a desire to meditate for themselves.

3. The expounding of the Scriptures leaves to the hearers a connecting link, so that reading over again the portion of the Word which has been expounded brings to their remembrance what has been said. Thus, with God's blessing, it leaves a more lasting impression on their minds.

4. The expounding of large portions of the Word, as the whole of a gospel or an epistle, besides leading the *hearer* to see the connection of the whole, has also this benefit for the teacher, that it leads him, with God's blessing, to the consideration of portions of the Word, which otherwise he might not have considered, and keeps him from speaking too much on favourite subjects, and leaning too much to

particular parts of truth, which tendency must surely sooner or later injure both himself and his hearers.

Expounding the Word of God brings little honour to the preacher from the unenlightened or careless hearer, but it tends much to the benefit of the hearers in general (N1, 1869).

What makes the truly great preacher

Simplicity of expression, while the truth is set forth, is of the utmost importance. It should be the aim of the teacher to speak so that children, servants, and people who cannot read may be able to understand him, so far as the natural mind can understand the things of God. If *they* can understand, the well-educated or literary persons will also understand; but the reverse does not hold good.

It ought also to be remembered that the expounder of the truth of God speaks for God, for eternity, and that it is not in the least likely that he will benefit the hearers, except he uses plainness of speech, which nevertheless needs not to be vulgar or rude.

It should also be considered that if the preacher strive to speak according to the rules of this world, he may please many, particularly those who have a literary taste; but, in the same proportion, he is less likely to become an instrument in the hands of God for the conversion of sinners or the building up of saints. For neither eloquence nor depth of thought make the truly great preacher, but such a life of prayer and meditation and spirituality as may render him a vessel meet for the Master's use, and fit to be employed both in the conversion of sinners and in the edification of the saints (N1, 1869).

Satan's power

The Holy Scriptures tell us of Satan being bound, yes, bruised under our feet; but this has not yet taken place. We are yet in the warfare, we constantly experience his power still. We have therefore for our comfort to lay hold on the blessings promised in this respect; and thus our hearts will be cheered and comforted (Y, 1869).

It is a common temptation of Satan to make us give up the reading of the Word and prayer when our enjoyment is gone; as if it were of no use to read the Scriptures when we do not enjoy them, and as if it were no use to pray when we have no spirit of prayer. The truth is that, in order to enjoy the Word, we ought to continue to read it, and the way to obtain a spirit of prayer is to continue praying. The less we read the Word of God, the less we desire to read it, and the less we pray, the less we desire to pray (N1, 1829).

Just like God

When all the expenses of the new Orphan House Number 1 had been met in full, I had a balance of more than six hundred pounds in hand; and when all the expenses for building, fitting up and furnishing Numbers 2 and 3 had been defrayed, there was about two thousand nine hundred pounds left. Thus the Lord showed that he could not only provide the large sums needed for these three orphan houses, but that He could also give more than was enough, and all simply in answer to prayer, though about sixty thousand pounds had been required.

In the same way, I expect that when all the expenses connected with the new Orphan Houses Numbers 4 and 5 shall have been defrayed there will be again a balance left. This is just like the ways of God. When He orders something to be done for the glory of His name, He is both able and willing to find the needed individuals for the work and the means required.

Thus, when the tabernacle in the wilderness was to be erected, He not only fitted men for the work, but He also touched the hearts of the Israelites to bring the necessary materials and gold, silver and precious stones. All these things were not only brought, but in such abundance that a proclamation had to be made in the camp that no more articles should be brought, because there were more than enough.

Again, when God for the praise of His name would have the temple to be built by Solomon, He provided such an amount of gold, silver, precious stones, brass and iron, that all the palaces that have been built since have been most insignificant in comparison with that temple (N3, 1869).

How heavenly realities become present things

'We live by faith, not by sight' (2 Cor. 5:7). As long as the child of God is in the world, he has not in actual possession what he will have when with the Lord, and especially what he will have after the return of the Lord Jesus. He is not yet what he then will be. He does not see what he then will see. But while we are yet in weakness, whilst in the body, in comparative ignorance, and have still to contend against mighty enemies, God has been pleased to give us a revelation of Himself in the Holy Scriptures to be our rule of action, to comfort and encourage us, to make Himself known to us, to make the Lord Jesus known to us, to tell us of the blessedness of the world to come, to show us the way to the Father's house, and to reveal to us the vanity of all that this present world can give.

This Word of God, the revelation He has been pleased to make of Himself, is to be credited, to be received fully, in childlike simplicity. In doing so, heavenly realities become present things to us by faith. We have not to judge by feeling, by seeing, by reasoning, but by believing – by exercising faith in what God says. Thus our ways and our actions are regulated; and thus our joys and sorrows (Y, 1869).

The presence of God

God is not seen by the natural eye. We have to seek to see Him, and to set Him before us daily, hourly, momentarily, by faith; and to bring Him and keep Him near to us by faith. The presence of God, the habitual presence of God, because we believe that He sees us and hears us continually, has to regulate our life.

We have to live in this world as those who would exercise faith in the truth that their heavenly Father is continually their Provider, their Protector, their Helper, their Friend; that He is ever near to them, that He is a wall of fire round about them continually.

If the child of God thus treated God, exercised faith in Him, looked upon Him practically as the living God ever near to Him, how peacefuly and happily would he walk through the world (Y, 1869).

Working for good

The testimony of God the Holy Spirit in Romans 8:28 is: 'And we know that in all things God works for the good of those who love him, who have been called according to his purpose.' Now if we lay hold on this truth by faith, bring to it in faith our greatest trials, difficulties, afflictions and bereavements, our hearts will be comforted, and we shall obtain peace to our souls.

I have been a believer in the Lord Jesus for forty-four years, but I have invariably found that my greatest trials have proved my greatest blessings; they have worked for my good. But suppose we did not see this to be so, while yet in the body, we have nevertheless to exercise faith concerning what God says. We have to walk by faith regarding that word of His that 'in all things God works for the good of those who love Him', and then will the heart be comforted and sustained (Y, 1869).

Becoming acquainted with God

Three years ago God allowed two most heavy trials to befall me. They continued month after month. I said to myself, 'This works for my good', and I continued day by day, while the afflictions lasted, to make known my requests unto God, that He would graciously be pleased to sustain me under them, and in His own time, deliver me out of them.

There was hanging in my bedroom in a frame a text, 'Open your mouth wide, and I will fill it' (Ps. 81:10), upon which my eyes fell as I rose in the morning. My heart said to my heavenly Father, 'I do open my mouth wide; will You graciously be pleased to do according to Your Word, and will You fill it?'

I continued patiently, believingly, expectingly, to look to God for help, and He did deliver me out of those two most heavy afflictions, and I have thus become further acquainted with Him.

All this I say for the comfort and encouragement of my younger brethren and sisters in Christ. Will you then, the next time you are in trial, seek to remember this for your comfort? You may not be able to see how such and such a heavy trial can work for your good; but it will most assuredly, as God has said. And if even in this life you should not see it, you will do so in the world to come; but generally we see it already in this life (Y, 1869).

Cast your cares upon the Lord

The reason why the children of God are so frequently overpowered by difficulties and trials is that they attempt to carry their burden themselves, instead of casting it upon God, as He not only graciously allows them to do, but commands them to do. Therefore they lose the promise which is coupled with the command and find themselves not sustained. 'Cast your cares upon the Lord and he will sustain you' (Ps. 55:22).

This does not mean simply that we should pray to God in our trials and afflictions, but that we should exercise faith in the power and willingness of God to help us under our trials. By this we know whether we have only used words in prayer, or whether we have, in *believing* prayer, exercising faith in God, spoken to Him about our trials. If the latter was the case, then, though the trial still lasts, the burden thereof is gone, because we have laid it upon God, to bear it for us. But if we have not exercised faith in God, we are still carrying the burden ourselves (Y, 1869).

Faith begins where sight fails

All these matters are so deeply important, because if we do not walk by faith we cannot be happy in God, and therefore cannot bear such a testimony for God as we should bear were we indeed happy. Our very countenance should testify to our peace and joy in God, in order that thus the unconverted may be stirred up to seek for themselves after that which makes the children of God so happy.

We have to believe what God says. Nor must we look to our feelings, nor expect help from our natural fallen reason. Nor must we be discouraged, though all appearances were against what God says; for faith begins where sight fails.

As long as we can see with the natural eye, and our natural fallen reason will help us, faith is not needed. This is often lost sight of by the children of God. Hence they are so much discouraged, because they do not walk by sight, which was never intended for them while they are yet in the body. If there is then one thing that we need more than another, it is an increase of faith, in order that we may take right steps, surer steps and firmer steps. We need to run with alacrity in the ways of the Lord. To the end of our course we need to pray, 'Lord increase my faith' (Y, 1869).

The blessings of a godly wife

Müller's first wife, Mary, died in February, 1870, aged seventy-two. Müller recalled –

I never saw my beloved wife, at any time when I met her unexpectedly in Bristol, without being delighted to do so. I never met her even in the orphan houses without my heart being delighted so to do. Day by day, as we met in our dressing room, at the orphan houses to wash our hands before lunch and tea, I was delighted to meet her, and she was equally pleased to see me.

Thousands of times I told her, 'My darling, I never saw you at any time, since you became my wife, without my being delighted to see you ' . . .

126

Our happiness in God, and in each other, was indescribable. We had not some happy days every year, nor a month of happiness every year; but we had twelve months of happiness in the year, and thus year after year. Often and often did I say to that beloved one, and this again even in the fortieth year of our marriage, 'My darling, do you think there is a couple in Bristol, or in all the world, happier than we are?'

Why do I refer to all this? To show what a remarkably great blessing to a husband is a truly godly wife, who also in other respects is fitted for him (N3, 1870).

Scriptural truths as realities not notions

The Sunday following Mary's death, Müller occupied the pulpit at Bethesda chapel as usual. During his address he said –

Last Lord's day, immediately after the death of my beloved wife, I should have been here if I had had physical strength. But having had to watch night after night for several nights, I was unable to come. Moreover I felt it my duty to my household to stay at home with them, for many reasons. But so far as the state of my heart was concerned, I should have been able as calmly and quietly to occupy this place as I do now.

Why do I refer to this? To seek to encourage you to acquaint yourselves with God – to know God. And I, by His grace, know Him, and find in Him such satisfaction, and I know there is in Him such love to me, that my soul is satisfied with Him.

See, therefore, the deep importance of coming to the Scriptures. For it is written, 'They that know your name will put their trust in you.' I know Him, therefore I put my trust in Him. But if you only hear about Him, or read about

Him, if you do not know Him as He has revealed Himself in the Scriptures, then, when trials and difficulties come, it will be seen how little you are acquainted with Him.

How important then that we hold the truth as it is in Jesus, that we know what God says about the vanities of this world, the blessedness of the world to come, and heavenly realities. Because my soul was enabled to lay hold on eternal life, to treat the truths of the Scriptures as realities, to grasp them by faith and not to hold them as notions, therefore in the midst of the storm I was calm and quiet, and there was not so much as a particle of difference between the bridal day and the funeral day. Oh, the holy calmness of my soul.

But you must know God. I delight to speak about Him, because our holy faith is a reality. The God of the Bible is the same in the second part of the nineteenth century as He was at the beginning. There is no difference between the living God four thousand years ago and now; no difference between what the blessed Jesus was when on earth and now. Only let us seek to acquaint ourselves with Him; only in child-like simplicity come to the Word and believe it, and lay hold on it (S, 1870).

Realising our oneness in Christ

From an opening address to a united prayer meeting in the Broadmead Rooms, Bristol, 1870, attended by Christians from all denominations –

We are invited to ask God's blessing on His work in Bristol. The particular point here is 'in Bristol'. Not at this church or this chapel; not at this Sunday-school or another Sunday-school; not in connection with particular movements of individual Christians, or city missionaries, or district visitors, but the work of God in Bristol. This at once brings before us that we are one in Christ, and all interested in His work that is going on around us.

Beloved in Christ, the realising our oneness in Christ may be tested by the extent to which we feel interested about the work of God that is going on in the hands of others. It is the will of the Lord that we should rejoice with those who rejoice; it is His will that we should weep with those who weep. If it please God to work a mighty work of conversion – though as to myself I had not the least to do with it – I ought to rejoice. If God is pleased to use individuals as instruments of blessing, though known only by name to me, I ought to rejoice in the work of God.

First, I am to give myself to pray for the work in which I am engaged, and to which God has been pleased to call me. But I am not to be satisfied with this. I ought to pray for the work of God in this city generally. Let me affectionately ask my fellow-believers whether they are in the habit of so doing? It is a solemn and important question.

If not, let me affectionately press this upon my fellow-believers, especially my younger brethren and sisters. I say – not boastingly, but simply to encourage my fellow-believers – that for many a long year I have been, day by day, praying for the work of God in Bristol – and not only in Bristol, but for the work of God in this neighbourhood, in this country, and throughout the world. Not a day passes without my bringing this matter before the Lord (I, 1870).

Buying the truth

What will help us, who believe in Christ, to be more united together? One might say, 'Oh, we must give up our differences.' Allow me affectionately and humbly to say I don't think so.

129

According to my judgment, a closer union would not be brought about by this means, by giving up our own views of what we consider to be taught us by God in the Scriptures. Not thus; but the great point is to hold them in their proper place, and to let the foundation truths of our holy faith have their proper place.

We have not to say, 'Now for this evening I will put aside all that I hold distinctively from my brethren.' No! Nor would I expect this from my brethren. We will, by God's grace, carry out the teaching of Scripture, 'Buy the truth and do not sell it' (Prov. 23:23). With diligence and prayerfulness, and, if necessary, great sacrifice, we ought to buy the truth; but having obtained it, for no price whatever is it to be sold, not even for our liberty or our life.

But beloved, while this is the truth, it is only one side of the truth. The other side is this: the foundation truths of our holy faith are so great, so momentous, and so precious, so altogether superabounding in comparison with anything else, that if we lived more under their influence, and more valued and enjoyed them, we should be constrained to love one another, to be knit together in love (I, 1870).

Loving those who differ from us

Now we know we have one and the same Saviour, therefore we are most intimately united in this. By this faith in the Lord Jesus we are all introduced into one family. Through this believing the Gospel, we become the children of God and all have one Father in Heaven, one Saviour. All are bought by the same precious blood, baptised by the Holy Spirit into one body, and are all walking the same road to Heaven.

If this were present in our hearts, I say, then this or that difference of opinion would not separate or alienate us. Let

130

me affectionately say, there is a blessedness and sweetness connected with really holding the membership of the body, and loving our fellow-believers, though we differ from them, that brings unspeakable joy to the soul. We should love our fellow-believers for Christ's sake, without asking to what portion of the Church of Christ they belong.

I ask just these questions, 'Are you a disciple of the Lord Jesus?' 'Do you love the Lord Jesus?' *This* must be settled. There can be no spiritual fellowship without *this*; but *that* being settled, no others should be raised (I, 1870).

Unity without uniformity

But it may be asked, 'Is it possible that, differing in this and that, brethren can be united together?'

They can. In the three orphan houses and six schools under my direction there are sixty teachers and other helpers. These are found belonging to the Church of England, Presbyterians, Independents, Baptists of close communion and open communion, Wesleyans of the Conference and of the Free Church parties, and of the so-called 'Brethren'. All these, though from different bodies of saints, are united together in this one object of labour for Christ.

During the many years we have been thus engaged, I have never known a jar to take place because of such difference. This does not arise from a sort of latitudinarianism in myself, but because, while holding firmly my own convictions, I have not required uniformity in these labourers.

In engaging my helpers, it is indispensable that they belong to the Head, that they hold fast the blessed Son of God. This settled, I never question as to what denomination they belong to. This is not brought forward boastingly, but to magnify the grace of God (K, 1863).

Imitating God

Why is it important to know more of God? Because it tends to holiness, happiness and usefulness.

It tends to holiness: the more I know of God, the more I am constrained to admire Him, and to say, 'What a lovely, good Being He is!' And especially when I see His wondrous love in Christ Jesus to such a guilty, wicked creature as I am; and therefore my heart is constrained to seek to imitate God, to seek to do something in return for His love, and to be more like God Himself.

It also tends to happiness: the more we know of God, the happier we are. It was when we were in entire ignorance of God that we were without real peace or joy. When we became a little acquainted with God, our peace and joy – our true happiness, I mean – commenced; and the more we become acquainted with Him, the more truly happy we become. What will make us so exceedingly happy in Heaven? It will be the fuller knowledge of God – we shall know Him then far better than we now do.

The knowledge of God tends to our usefulness in His service here: it is impossible that I can enter into what God has done for sinners, without being constrained in return to seek to live for Him, to labour for Him. I ask myself, 'What can I do for Him who has bestowed upon me His choicest gifts?'

Hence I am constrained to labour for Him. According to the measure in which I am fully acquainted with God, do I seek to labour for Him. I cannot be idle (I, 1870).

How to read the Bible

What is the best way of reading the Scriptures? I say a little about this, because in my experience in pastoral labour I have found how deeply important it is to know how to read the Scriptures; and because, after forty years' blessed experience, I can confidently recommend the plan I have adopted.

In the first place, in order to have a deeper acquaintance with the Scriptures, it is absolutely needful that you read the whole in course, regularly through – not as some perhaps do, take the Bible, and where it opens there begin to read. If it opens at Psalm 102, they read Psalm 102; if at John 14, or Romans 8, they read John 14 or Romans 8. By degrees the Bible opens naturally on such portions. Let me affectionately say that it ill becomes the child of God thus to treat the Father's Book; it ill becomes the disciples of the Lord Jesus thus to treat their blessed Master.

Let me affectionately urge those who have not done so, to begin the Old Testament from the beginning, and the New Testament from the beginning; at one time reading in the Old, and at another time in the New Testament, keeping a mark in their Bible to show how far they have proceeded. Why is it important to do this?

There is a special purpose in the arrangement of the Scriptures. They begin with the creation of the world, and close with the end of the world. As you read a book of biography or history, commencing at the beginning and reading through to the end, so should you read the revelation of God's will. And when you get to the end, begin again at the beginning (I, 1870).

Something of real good to you

But this is not all that is necessary. When you come to this blessed Book, the great point is to come with a deep consciousness of your own ignorance, seeking on your knees the help of God, that by His Spirit He may graciously instruct you.

I remember when I thus began to read the Scriptures. I had been a student of divinity in the University of Halle, and had written many a long manuscript at the lectures of

the professors of divinity; but I had not come to this blessed
Book in the right spirit.

At length I came to it as I had never done before. I said,
'The Holy Spirit is the Teacher now in the Church of Christ;
the Holy Scriptures are now the rule given by God; from
them I must learn His mind. I will now prove it.'

I locked my door. I put my Bible on the chair. I fell down
before the chair, and spent three hours prayerfully reading
the Word of God. I unhesitatingly say that in those three
hours I learned more than in any previous three, six, or
twelve months' period of my life. This was not all. I not only
increased in knowledge, but there came with that
knowledge a peace and joy in the Holy Spirit of which I had
known little before.

Since that time, for more than forty years, I have been in
the habit of regularly reading the Scriptures. I can affectionately and confidently recommend to my beloved younger fellow-disciples to read them carefully, with an humble
mind, comparing Scripture with Scripture, bringing the
more difficult passages to the easy ones, and letting them
interpret one another. If you do not understand some
portions, be not discouraged, but come again and again to
God, and He will guide you by little and little, and further
instruct you in the knowledge of His will. But this is not all;
for with an increasing knowledge of God, obtained in a
prayerful, humble way, you will receive, not something
which simply fills the head, but something which exercises
the heart, and cheers, comforts and strengthens you, and
will therefore be of real good to you (I, 1870).

Depending entirely on the power of the Holy Spirit

The Holy Spirit was given on the day of Pentecost to the
Church in her collective capacity, to abide with her forever,
and has not been taken away, notwithstanding our many

failings. Just as the fiery pillar was not taken from the Israelites, notwithstanding their many provocations, so the blessed Spirit of God has not been taken away from the Church. Moreover God has given His Spirit to the individual believer – to all who put their trust in the Lord Jesus Christ.

But though the Spirit dwells in the Church of Christ as to her collective capacity, and in the individual believer, nevertheless it is fitting and suitable and right on the part of the children of God that they should ask God again and again, and with great earnestness, that He would work mightily by His Spirit.

We depend entirely on the power of the Holy Spirit for the conversion of sinners. There might be the most mighty preacher as to the knowledge of the Scriptures and the clearness with which he sets forth the truth; yet if the Spirit of God is not pleased to bless the Word, he may preach for months, and yet there will be no blessing (I, 1870).

The sovereignty of God

From an address given at Salem chapel, Bristol, at a Monday evening prayer meeting in September, 1870 –

It was forty-four years ago, on the 17th of the month, that I began to preach in my own country. But I saw very little fruit from my preaching. I preached in the parish churches – I loved to preach, there was a real earnestness in my preaching, and a real desire to do good – unquestionably so; and yet I never met with a single instance in which I could say I had been used as God's instrument in the conversion of a sinner, though sometimes I preached to a thousand people or more. I do not say that persons may not have been converted – but I never met with one single instance of conversion.

In course of time I came to this country, and it pleased God then to show me the doctrines of grace [i.e., the sovereignty of God, election] in a way in which I had not seen them before. At first I hated them and said, 'If this were true, *I* could do nothing at all in the conversion of sinners, as all would then depend upon God and the working of His Spirit.'

But when it pleased God to reveal these truths to me, and my heart was brought to such a state that I could say, 'I am not only content simply to be a hammer, an axe, or a saw in God's hands, but I shall count it an honour to be taken up and used by Him in any way. If sinners are converted through my instrumentality, from my inmost soul I will give Him all the glory.'

The Lord gave me to see fruit in abundance. Sinners were converted by scores, and ever since God has used me in one way or another in His service (H, 1870).

Giving God the glory

I delight to dwell on this, especially for the benefit of my younger fellow-believers. We must be willing to give God all the glory. We may say, 'God shall have all the glory' but the point is, do we mean it? We must aim after this, to be content to be nothing but the instrument, giving God all the glory. We must not say, 'God shall have ninety-nine parts of the glory, and the one-hundredth part shall be ours.' No, we must give Him all, we must not take the one-hundredth part; He is worthy to have it all.

Let us aim after this, and assuredly God will take us up; for He can then use us. Our adorable Lord Jesus, during all His life on earth, had one single aim – to seek glory for the Father. Well, as we are enabled to get glory for the Master, not for the servant, so He, whom we seek to honour, will see to it that honour is bestowed on the servant.

136

I affectionately, as an elder brother, lay it upon the hearts of my beloved young brethren, whether engaged as preachers, Sunday-school teachers, tract distributors, home visitors, or in any other way working in the Lord's service, if they desire to see fruit resulting from their labours, that they primarily aim after this – that not only with the lip, but with the heart, they will give all the honour and glory to God, if He should condescend to use them as instruments in His service (H, 1870).

The humanity and divinity of Christ

Isaiah 9:6. 'For to us a child is born, to us a son is given, and the government will be on his shoulders. And he will be called Wonderful Counsellor, Mighty God, Everlasting Father, Prince of Peace.' This verse brings before us both the humanity and the divinity of our adorable Lord Jesus Christ. And we, the disciples of the Lord Jesus, should hold fast the true humanity and the true divinity of our adorable Lord.

We have to seek practically, day by day, to enter into the truth, that He who is at the right hand of the Father – the ascended living Lord Jesus Christ – is, in the presence of God, still the God-Man. He is our brother in the presence of God. But that blessed One, who is our Saviour, at the same time is not only truly man, but is really and truly God, as fully as is the Father. Of this truth, that He is very Man and very God – the God-Man – we have to seek to remind ourselves continually.

For there will come a time when we shall need to remember the truth in both these aspects – His true humanity and true divinity. I would say to any who are not aware of it, that 750 years before the incarnation of our adorable Lord, the Holy Spirit, by Isaiah, made the statement contained in the verse above. How this in itself is calculated to refresh our hearts, and strengthen us in the belief that this blessed Book, the Bible, is the Word of the living God! (L, 1870).

Jesus the Counsellor

How full of comfort is the word 'Counsellor' as applied to our Lord. We shall find ourselves, in our course heaven-wards, again and again in positions when we particularly need counsel and advice. Now the blessed Lord Jesus – our Brother, our Friend, our Saviour, our Lord, our God – sustains the office of the Counsellor to His Church, and to His individual disciples. To myself I ought to say, when in perplexing circumstances, 'Oh, let me lie in the bosom of the Lord Jesus.' To Him let me pray, 'Your poor servant knows not how to act, knows not what to do, but you are the Counsellor of your people; now prove yourself in my happy experience my Counsellor!'

What would be the result? As assuredly as we exercise faith in the Lord Jesus Christ with regard to this His office, and as assuredly as we give ourselves to prayer, and seek, by the Spirit of God, through the instrumentality of the written Word, to obtain counsel of Him, so assuredly we shall obtain it (L, 1870).

Jesus the mighty God

Then, when in weakness as to the outward man, or in weakness spiritually, in any difficulty, in any trial, or any sorrow, when we are in the hour of temptation, needing special help, how blessed to remember 'the mighty God', to remember He is the mighty God.

There is no question as to this being the meaning of it. Every word in Isaiah 9:6 is honestly translated. The greatest Hebrew scholars, though rationalists, were constrained to acknowledge that that was the meaning, and they have translated the words thus. How full they are of comfort!

He, my Friend, my Lord, my Saviour, my Bridegroom, is the mighty God. *I* am perfect weakness, *I* cannot stand against my enemies, *I* am helpless. Oh, how weak, how extremely weak am *I* in myself! But if I cling to the mighty God, He is able and willing to help me. He proved the depth of His love to me by laying down His life for me, a miserable guilty sinner. He, our best friend, our bosom Friend, is at the same time the mighty God. Oh! let us cling to the mighty God (L, 1870).

What a lovely Being Jesus is!

From an address to an Annual Conference of Christians at Clifton –

While all things change here below, the precious Jesus, our Friend, is 'the same yesterday, and today, and forever'. What He was millions of years ago, He is now. What He was when He walked through Judaea, Samaria, and Galilee, He is now – His heart full of tenderness, of pity, of compassion. Oh, how patient, how loving, how gracious! Oh, what a lovely Being Jesus is!

When I saw the notice of these Conference meetings, I was particularly refreshed by the remembrance of this – that Jesus will be the theme again of our meetings. I have been privileged to attend every one of these evening meetings during the eight years they have been held, and Jesus, Jesus, Jesus, has been the theme of every meeting. Well now, beloved fellow-disciples, it should be Jesus, Jesus, Jesus, more practically and experimentally in our closets, in our walk, in our labour, in our service; and day by day our hearts should be occupied with Jesus, and especially the friendship of Jesus should be cultivated by us increasingly. When trials, difficulties, and sorrows come, we should remember we have the same Jesus now as ready to comfort and encourage us as He did the disciples more than 1800 years ago. He is quite as ready as He was then to prove Himself our Friend, our Helper, our Comforter (L, 1870).

What God has provided for us in Jesus

We should say, 'Now Lord Jesus, since you are "the same yesterday, and today, and forever", and since it is written that you have "the tongue of the learned" to "know how to speak a word in season to him that is weary", give me a word in season to comfort me. You are willing, now comfort me, your poor servant, for I am weary. You are ever the same, and since you are willing to comfort now as you were in Judaea, in Samaria, and Galilee, now comfort me your poor servant.'

Thus should we prove Jesus practically and experimentally to be our bosom friend. And we should seek to couple with the experience that He is our bosom friend the fact that He is the mighty God, and ever the same. If all my friends fail, this precious Jesus remains, and He will never forsake, He will never grow weary, He will ever care for me. How full of comfort is this!

Let us enter into what God, in the riches of His grace, has been pleased to provide for us in Jesus. There is reality in

140

these things. God brings this precious truth before us that we may be sustained and comforted. And if practically and experimentally we lean on the arm of Christ, it shall be yet seen in these last days how happy the disciples of the Lord Jesus may be, though everything be dark and gloomy, and though they are in the midst of difficulties and trial.

Not only this – we may even be strong in the Lord; and whilst we cannot be apostles, we may aim after the grace of apostles. Though we never attain to it, it would be a holy aim, and God would be pleased with it. In ourselves we are perfect weakness; yet the Holy Spirit is in the Church, and dwells in every individual believer, and we have the written Word, and Jesus our bosom friend. Therefore if we pour out our hearts before God, in the midst of all our difficulties and trials, what strength may we not get to our souls? Let us live on Jesus, beloved in Christ (L, 1870).

The King in His beauty

I refer to the bright and blessed prospect both with regard to the coming of our Lord Jesus Christ, when Himself shall put aside war, Himself shall take the power and reign, and all the kingdoms of the world shall become the kingdoms of the Christ of God; when the blessed Jesus will come, not in the character in which He came before, but 'as the King in His beauty'.

How the heart, with joyful anticipation, should look forward to the day when He will come and reign, and take the power to Himself, and subdue everything that is contrary to Himself. This is the bright and blessed prospect before us, and most blessed with regard to our own hearts now. He will subdue in us individually everything contrary to His own blessed mind. The Lord Jesus will have His own blessed mind to the full seen in us. Precious, bright,

141

glorious the prospect! After waiting yet a little while, we shall see Jesus as He is, and be made like Him (L, 1870).

The timing of Christ's return

Now for this blessed One – for the personal return of this blessed One – we have to wait. He said before He ascended: 'If I go and prepare a place for you, I will come back and take you to be with me that you also may be where I am' (John 14:3). We all know He did go to the Father; but He will not be satisfied till He returns to take His Church to Himself, that where He is, she may be also.

As to the time when this will take place, what can we say? If we attempt to say it will be next month, it will be next year, we should not stand on scriptural ground; for it is written, 'No-one knows about that day or hour, not even the angels in Heaven' (Matt. 24:36).

I well remember the mistake into which many fell about the time when it pleased God first to reveal to me the truth with regard to the return of the Lord. In July 1829, as many will remember, there was war between Russia and the Ottoman Empire. Many beloved brethren, whose minds had just been opened to look for the return of their Lord, said, 'Now is the time when Israel will be restored. You will see,' they said, 'in a short time how all this Turkish Empire will be destroyed.' Having my mind recently directed to the subject of our Lord's return, I fell into the same mistake as many of my elder brethren.

What was the result? Six weeks more, and peace was restored between Russia and the Turkish Empire; forty-one years and seven months have passed since then, and the Turkish Empire still exists, and Israel has not been restored (X, 1870).

Interpreting the signs

Why do I refer to this? Not to indicate that we are not to look at the circumstances around us. It is the will of the Lord that we should do so, and not shut our eyes to what is passing around us. But this I affectionately say, that we should not be too hasty in forming a judgment that because a certain event has taken place, therefore at a particular time it is certain the Lord Jesus will return. Otherwise, when the time shall have passed, and after all our adorable Lord Jesus has not been revealed, unbelievers may turn round and say, 'The time has passed, and the Lord Jesus, of Whose return you talked so much, has not come; and after all, is there anything in the truth about His return?'

We should be careful not to give a handle to those who speak evil of the truth; and not lay too much stress on certain events which may not be God's instruments in ushering in the return of the Lord (X, 1870).

Never go into debt

We still, as from the beginning of the institution, never go in debt for anything. The reason why we refrain from doing so is because it would otherwise appear as if God were too poor to pay for His own work. If our work is indeed the *work of God*; and if indeed *we* are the individuals to do this work for Him; and if, lastly, *His time* is come, when we shall do this work for Him, He will surely make it manifest that we are not mistaken by supplying us with the needed means.

But the work we are engaged in may not be according to His mind; if so, we cannot be surprised that He does not give us the means. Or, though the work is according to His mind, *we* may not be the persons who He means to use in His work; and, therefore, He may withhold from us the

143

means. Or lastly, though the work is the work which pleases God, and though we are also the individuals whom He will condescend to use in doing this work, His time may not have come for our doing this work.

What, then, have we to do under such circumstances? Shall we seek anyhow to obtain the means? Shall we, by our way of acting, appear to say that we know better than God? We ought not. It becomes us rather to wait God's own time, which will bring blessing to our own souls; which will prove that we are true servants of the Master, because we wait on Him. Thus it will be useful to our fellow-disciples (N3, 1870).

Walking in friendship with God

October 8, 1872. . . . While I am writing this, the income during the last five days has been so small that it would not cover the fifth part of the expenses of these five days. But I am again expecting larger sums.

It is unspeakably blessed really to know God, to walk in friendship with Him, to be able to speak to Him about everything, and to roll upon Him all one's cares and burdens. In this blessed, happy way I have now been enabled to walk for 44 years, and I cannot describe the joy connected with this life of holy, blessed independence of circumstances, political events, mercantile difficulties, friends and death. As long as we are able to lean upon God, we have all we can possibly need. All this blessed holy independence may be enjoyed by all the children of God. It is not only the privilege of a very few favoured ones; but all, without exception, who are reconciled to God, by faith in the Lord Jesus, and who alone trust in Him for salvation, may enjoy this blessing.

In order however to enjoy this happy fellowship and practical friendship of God and His dear Son, our adorable

Lord Jesus Christ, we must walk uprightly. We have to carry out the light which we receive from the Holy Scriptures. We must practise the truth we know. Erring and failing we must be, but we must be honest, upright in not living in sin, in not going on in a course we know to be contrary to the mind of God. If we live like this we shall not be able practically to trust Him as a friend, and this will be the greatest hindrance to having our prayers answered, according to that word: 'If I had cherished sin in my heart, the Lord would not have listened' (Ps. 66:18), (J, 1872).

Eyes directed towards the Lord . . .

Our requirements are great and many, and regarding them all we have our eyes directed towards the Lord, and He is mindful of us, though sometimes faith and patience are considerably exercised, before the needed help comes. Here, however, I will now more particularly refer to our financial needs, received from the hands of our loving, gracious, God and Father.

The reader therefore will kindly place himself in our position during the year with more than two thousand persons, day by day, sitting down to meals. The expense of this alone, as everyone can suppose, is great, during one year only, especially if it be remembered how great the price of all kinds of provisions has been and is, and how very dear our coal is.

But these two thousand orphans are not only to be fed but clothed; their clothes are to be washed and repaired. The one single article of boots and shoes alone, think of it, for two thousand, both the supplies of new and repairs: how many hundred pounds it takes!

Hundreds of fresh orphans are received year by year, and the new comers are to be fitted out; hundreds of boys and girls go out as apprentices and servants, and they are to be provided with an outfit at the expense of the institution. The considerable number of boys who are sent out as apprentices, year by year, have a premium paid for them to their masters, which is about equal to another year's support.

Then come the heavy expenses connected with keeping in repair these five large houses, in which there are more than seventeen hundred large windows and above five hundred rooms. This is only mentioned to give the reader, who has not seen the houses, an idea of their magnitude (N3, 1872).

. . . The infinitely rich one

It may therefore easily be supposed how much the mere painting, white-washing, colouring and repairs must cost year by year! Then consider the many thousands of articles of table linen, bed linen and towels – all has to be kept up! The thousands of articles of furniture in these more than five hundred rooms have to be kept in repair, or to be replaced by new articles.

The children are ill, or one or the other even dies – all the extra expenses are to be met. The children leave as servants or apprentices – the travelling expenses are to be paid. Further, remember the large staff of overseers of one kind or another, such as school inspectors, matrons, teachers, medical officers, assistants helping the directors and so on – all their salaries are to be obtained from the Lord. All the nurses in the infirmaries in each of the five houses, the nurses for the little infants, the laundresses and other servants – all this costs much, and for all this we look to the Lord. And there are, over and above, year by year, heavy extra expenses not here referred to, occasioned by extraordinary circumstances, for all of which we look to the Lord.

May this suffice to give the reader a faint idea of our

position with regard to the orphan work alone, and he will readily see that it not only requires the purse of a nobleman, but that at least nine out of ten of our nobility would be unable to meet these expenses year by year, and that only a few of the most wealthy could do so. But we have nothing of their wealth, and yet are we able with as much ease, if not greater ease than very rich noblemen, to accomplish this, simply by looking in our poverty to the infinitely rich one for everything (N3, 1872).

Making known the unsearchable riches of Christ . . .

It is an awful consideration that the vast majority of our fellow-men have never yet had the light of the Gospel, have never had salvation through faith in the atoning death of the Lord Jesus Christ preached to them. Have we sufficiently pondered this? Has it had a practical effect upon our lives? And what effect has it had?

1. Has it led to earnestness in prayer? Day by day we should pray that God would abundantly bless the labours of all His servants who preach the Gospel at home and abroad. Every day that we neglect this, we neglect what, as believers in the Lord Jesus, we ought to attend to. But we should also pray for those who are engaged in preaching the Gospel at home and abroad, that they may be upheld and strengthened, both as to their outward and inward man.

2. But, if we are sincere in our prayer, we shall do more than this. Perhaps we can give ourselves to this service – of making known the unsearchable riches of Christ for the remainder of our lives. At least we should offer ourselves for this to the Lord. Should He not accept us for this, so that our earthly occupation is to be given up, we may be able to

give at least a part of our time to this service, though it were only in a more private way. But could even this not be done, every disciple of the Lord Jesus should at least embrace every opportunity offered to him by His Lord to point out the way of salvation to his friends, his relatives and others with whom he may come into contact. And every believer ought to aim after this, that he in his life and deportment commends the truth (N4, 1873).

. . . and practising self-denial

3. Are all believers considering that there is an obligation laid on them by the Lord to seek to help those who, as missionaries in foreign lands, or as evangelists at home, have given themselves to the service of seeking to spread abroad the way of salvation through the crucified and risen Lord Jesus? How can we suppose that we love the Lord Jesus, if we do not practically show our interest in the labours of those who, often with their lives in their hands, seek to spread the Gospel to which we owe our spiritual life, peace, joy, yes everything with reference to eternal realities?

Now what are we doing to help these missionaries and evangelists? How much of our time do we devote to them? What self-denial in the way of dress, luxury, pleasure, or sight-seeing do we practise on their account? Do we all spend as much as a twentieth part of our income for this object? Let us examine ourselves, let us be honest to our own hearts! Life will soon have come to an end. Our one brief life will soon be over. And then, in the retrospect of that one brief life here on earth, shall we be able to say that we did what we could (generally speaking) to help to spread the Gospel?

I fear many beloved true disciples of the Lord Jesus do very little with respect to missionary operations. Let us be earnest about this matter. There are openings in abundance for helping preachers of the Gospel.

4. If these various points were attended to, the beloved disciples of the Lord Jesus would be more abundantly blessed in their own souls, and would be to a greater extent used by the Lord. Moreover we should see the number of missionaries and evangelists not only greatly increased, but their labours would be far more abundantly blessed than they have been hitherto (N4, 1873).

'Mr Müller is a happy man'

It would pain me to the utmost if people could live with me a month in the house and not bear this testimony, that Müller is 'a happy man'. And a happy man I desire to be; and a happy man I am. It is Christ who makes me happy; for there is something unspeakably blessed in this – that the older one gets, the nearer the end of the journey, the brighter the blessedness of the prospect; with Heaven as one's home, that one is getting nearer and nearer to the gates.

Oh! How blessed to be in Christ. And this blessedness I desire for all my beloved dear young friends to whom I am especially speaking this evening. It is a blessed thing to be a believer in the Lord Jesus (C, 1873).

'There's the mystic!'

From an address to young men –

My dear young friends, let me tell you of the blessedness of being a believer in the Lord Jesus Christ. Only be an out and out Christian. It is this half-hearted mind which makes men unhappy. You cannot be happy if you want to hold the world with one hand and Christ with the other. But the moment you decide that you will not halt between two opinions, and that you will be an out and out Christian, you will be happy.

I know the difficulty of this, for when I was converted I was almost the only believer out of 1260 young men who were students at the university. They knew me, that I had been fencing, in order that I might be able to fight a duel if anyone insulted me. They knew me: 'There's the mystic!' as I was called, and they pointed their fingers at me. But these sneers lasted a few days or a few weeks at the most. By the grace of God, I stood by the side of Christ with two or three students out of 1260, and the result was, a happy man I was. And the result has been, a happy man I have been. But it must be an out and out thing (C, 1873).

Are you renewed by the Holy Spirit?

This is the momentous point, whether through faith in the Lord Jesus Christ we are partakers of the Holy Spirit or not. If any man have not the Spirit of Christ he is none of His. Whatever we have, if we have not the Holy Spirit, we do not belong to Christ. In whatever way we may seek to resemble the disciples of the Lord Jesus Christ – we may be in the habit of reading our Bibles, of bowing our knees, of singing together with them, of meeting together with them, of partaking with them at the Lord's supper, we may be reckoned among them as disciples – and yet with all this, far from God. With all this, unregenerate. With all this, wanting the Spirit of Christ. With all this, not born again through faith in the Lord Jesus Christ.

Talkers we may be, in outward appearance like the children of God, but if the heart is unrenewed, if there be no faith in the Lord Jesus Christ for the salvation of our souls, through which we are born again and renewed by the power of the Holy Spirit, so that the Holy Spirit takes our bodies and makes them His temple – if this is not the case, we are yet far from God and His kingdom (P, 1874).

Form or reality?

The solemn, momentous question, particularly in these days of almost universal profession and discipleship, when there is so much profession and religion in the land, is whether it is the form or the reality; whether we are born again, or yet dead in trespasses and sins with all our profession; whether merely in the way of form we bow the knee, and sing His praise, and say Amen to the prayers of others; or whether the heart goes along with the praises and prayers, or whether we only go to this or that meeting, because it is respectable in these days.

In the days of the apostles they were cast out as mad; but in these days no man is called a respectable man if he does not make a profession of religion in some shape; and people therefore in order that they may be respected would take a profession of some sort or other; and therefore the momentous question is this – Whether it is a reality? Whether it is heart work? Whether we be born again? Whether it is, after all, only a mere hollow profession?

The question is not whether my name is written on the Church book, but whether it is written in the Lamb's book of life; not how my fellow-men look on me, but how God looks on me (P, 1874).

The believer's happiness

God has not failed me at any time. Forty years have I proved His faithfulness in this work; and it is about thirty-six years ago when great poverty and need came upon me, in connection with this work, that the Lord in the most marked and manifest manner stretched forth His hand, as has been described in this Narrative. This almost uninterrupted poverty continued for five years; but God always helped me.

During the last twenty years, generally, His dealings have been different; still, even during this period, I have had numberless spiritual and temporal necessities to bring before God in prayer, and he has uniformly helped me. This same peace and joy in God, resulting from becoming increasingly acquainted with Him, by waiting upon Him, looking to Him, trusting in Him in the greatest difficulties, and under the greatest trials, and even when there is not the least natural prospect of being helped, I desire that you dear reader may have. The life of the believer in the Lord Jesus is intended to be a very happy one, even here on earth. But this cannot be, except you walk as an obedient child, and confide fully in your Father.

I cannot tell you how happy this service makes me. Instead of being the anxious careworn man many persons think me to be, I have no anxieties and no cares at all. Faith in God leads me to roll *all* my burdens upon Him; for hundreds are my necessities, besides those connected with money. In every way I find God to be my helper, even as I trust in Him, and pray to Him in child-like simplicity about everything. Be encouraged, dear fellow-believer, to go this blessed way yourself, and you will see what peace and joy it affords (N3, 1874).

How to conduct Christian work according to the faith principle

All these four points need carefully to be attended to.

In the first place, we have to be sure that the work in which we are engaged is really the *work of the Lord*, and fully so. I lay stress on this because I have seen how, in order to keep persons from certain evil things, there have been substituted other evil things which, though in the sight of some they may be less objectionable, yet are of such a character as that they are unworthy of the name of God's work. How then could help be expected from God under such circumstances?

Next we have to be sure that *we* are the persons to be engaged in that work, which is really God's work. For we are not our own, we are bought with a price, the precious blood of the Lord Jesus. We therefore may not spend our time, our talents, our bodily, mental and spiritual strength as we please. We have to seek to know whether the Lord would have us to be engaged in such and such a way or not. But even this is not enough.

We have still further to seek to find out, by patient waiting upon God, watching His hand, whether *His time* is come, that we should do this His work.

How important these last two points are, we have clearly shown to us in the building of the temple. The work was a good work, and quite according to the mind of Jehovah. But His time was not yet come that this work was to be done, when David desired to build the temple; nor was he to be the man to do it, but his son Solomon.

Suppose now lastly that the work is not only God's work, but that we are also the persons to be engaged in that work, and that His own time is come when we are to be engaged in this His work, we have lastly to trust in Him for all the help we need. If we do not do so, how could we expect to go on well (N4, 1875).

Simply praying will not do

How may I know whether I have cast my burden upon God? One says, 'By prayer!' Well, right or wrong, just as you understand it.

153

Right, if it is believing prayer, if you exercise faith in the power and willingness of God to carry the burden for you. But simply praying will not do.

We know we have rolled our burden upon God, if after praying, the heart is easy, the heart is light. If this is not the case, then we are still carrying the burden ourselves, instead of casting it upon God, and have need to go again to Him, and in believing prayer exercise faith with regard to the power and willingness of God to carry the burden for us (D, 1876).

Love shown me in all quarters

From an account to his own congregation of a preaching tour –

The first place visited in Scotland was Kilmarnock. The largest parish church, holding 1800, was placed at my disposal by the aged minister, a true evangelical man. I preached there three times; also preached in two different free churches, the church of the Evangelical Union, and the meeting place of the so-called Brethren – seven times altogether; also once at Saltcoats. Everywhere we were received with the greatest kindness. I was known everywhere; everywhere I was loved and esteemed. Hearts were opened, and pulpits were opened with delight.

This I felt to be the finger of God pointing out what was His will regarding me. I had reason to believe it would be so, for my heart has been towards the Church of Christ for many a year. I love all who love the Lord Jesus Christ, and I was loved among all the denominations, and by them all received with open arms, and the greatest kindness shown by everyone – by Episcopalians, National Churches, United Presbyterians, Morrisonians, Congregationalists,

Baptists and so-called Brethren – nothing but love shown me in all quarters!

... Brethren have told me, 'Well, we will go and tell a certain minister in the way of respect, but there is no prospect he will let you preach.' The reply has been, 'Is that Mr Müller of Bristol? Mr Müller of the orphan houses? Delighted to let him preach.' Such a thing never heard of before. Thus you see the openings God gives in every direction, and I feel a responsibility to use them (B, 1876).

Admiring the holiness of God

Psalm 103:1. 'Praise the Lord, O my soul; all my inmost being, praise his holy name.' This is only what believers can be engaged in. Naturally we care not about the holiness of God. Naturally, man likes to please himself, and would have God to be like himself. The attribute of holiness is the last, naturally, we care about. But when we are born again, when we are renewed, when we have spiritual life, there is born in our hearts a longing after holiness, and we rejoice in the fact that God is a holy Being.

Then we have a prospect of one day being like Him. Only a child of God takes a real interest in admiring the holiness of God, and rendering praise to Him for it.

The Psalmist adds in the second verse, 'Praise the Lord, O my soul, and forget not all his benefits.' We are in danger of forgetting the mercies of God. We are ready to speak about our trials, our difficulties, our bereavements, our crosses. But are we just as ready to speak of and admire the goodness of God, and His mercies in numberless ways bestowed upon us all the days of our life? This the Psalmist was particularly anxious about (F, 1876).

The most precious blessing you can have

Psalm 103:3. 'He forgives all my sins . . . ' Is this not the choicest blessing we have received? Is there one single blessing to be compared with this? What are all business blessings – and they are something to be grateful for – in comparison with the forgiveness of our sins? What are all the peace and quietness in the family – and these too are something to be grateful for – compared with the forgiveness of our sins? What is the soundness of the health of the body – for which we should be thankful – in comparison with the forgiveness of our sins? What is the vigour and strength of mind with which we are blessed in comparison with the forgiveness of our sins? It is as nothing in comparison with it. The Psalmist brings this blessing first because it is the choicest, the chiefest, and the most precious a human being can have (F, 1876).

Forgiveness, faith and works

Now God looks to us not to do something to complete the work of salvation, but to accept what He so graciously provides for the sinner in the person of His Son, whose righteousness He accepts for the sinner. But when the sinner believes in the Lord Jesus Christ, a different life begins: he seeks to please Christ, he seeks to adorn His doctrine, he seeks to walk according to His mind. He does this not to be saved thereby, or to add to the work of the Lord Jesus Christ. But having through faith been saved, having obtained forgiveness, and having been accepted in the righteousness of the Lord Jesus Christ wrought out for sinners, he seeks to please God. This is the way to obtain forgiveness – simply trusting in Jesus, thus believing in Jesus. Whoever does this obtains forgiveness (F, 1876).

Never a single minute's doubt in fifty years

The Psalmist does not say that *some* of your sins are forgiven but all. That is so precious. It is not that five hundred of our sins are forgiven, or five thousand, but every one; so that though they be innumerable, every one is forgiven. Just think – vile, guilty as we are, every sin of every one who believes in the Lord Jesus Christ is forgiven.

Do you enjoy it? I do enjoy the forgiveness of my sins. Not because I have very strong feelings. I do not rest on feelings. I take God at His word. I rest on His Word: 'Whoever believes in him shall not perish but have eternal life.' I believe in Jesus, therefore I have been pardoned. I have had no dream or vision about it. Some people think that unless by some strange vision or other they see Jesus suspended on the cross in some corner of the room they must remain in doubt. I have had no such vision. For fifty years I have never had a single minute's doubt about the forgiveness of my sins.

For these years I have been a believer, and all this time the Word I have referred to, and on which I rest, has been written in the Book, and by it I know my sins are forgiven (F, 1876).

No trifling with sin

Every believer who is willing to take God at His word has a right to look on himself as a pardoned sinner, as a forgiven sinner. This is a blessing, a great blessing to know that all our sins are forgiven.

Suppose now our sins are just 9090, and suppose we had the forgiveness of 9089 – just one single sin unforgiven. What then? This one single sin would bring us to the place of perdition. There is no trifling with sin. We must be perfectly without sin, hiding ourselves in the merits of the Lord Jesus Christ, and fully pardoned; or we are unclean, and cannot come into His presence.

Therefore see the blessedness of the statement of the Psalmist: 'Who forgives *all* my sins.' All gone! Oh, the blessedness of this! Every one gone! Sins of action, sins of word, sins of thought, sins of feeling, sins of desire, sins of purpose, sins of inclination – all gone, as assuredly as we put our trust in the Lord Jesus Christ for the salvation of our souls (F, 1876).

Christ's hospital

' . . . and heals all my diseases' (Ps. 103.3). This is the next blessing of which the Psalmist desired to be mindful. Here we do not mean to say that the diseases of the body are excluded; for if anyone is cured of any bodily disease, it is not by the skill of the doctor, or by the powerful character of the medicine, but by the blessing of God on the skill of the doctor.

Still I judge that the especial point referred to here is spiritual disease. You remember what Isaiah said in the beginning of his prophecies: 'From the sole of your foot to the top of your head there is no soundness – only wounds and welts and open sores.' We all know that he did not refer to the bodies of the Israelites, that they were not in the loathsome state as regarded the body, but that the reference was to their spiritual diseases.

That is the case with regard to all sinners at all times, and under all circumstances. If we are pure spiritually, it must come from the Lord. Now we have here particularly to remember that the poor sinner who trusts in the Lord Jesus Christ, the moment he does so is unconsciously, as it were, putting himself under the infinitely wise and gracious Physician. That blessed one takes him up and puts him into His own hospital, His own infirmary, and will not let him go till he is perfectly cured.

As you all know, there is no such thing as a discharge out of that hospital on account of incurable disease, as is commonly the case among men; but the patient is cared for till he is perfectly free from spiritual disease. The moment we are there the cure is going on (F, 1876).

Just like Jesus

And this is the prospect of the weakest: that as assuredly as he believes in Jesus, as assuredly as he is not living in sin, so assuredly will he be brought finally into that state in which he will be altogether free from sin. We have been apprehended of God to be conformed to the image of His Son, to be at last altogether like Him, altogether holy, altogether free from spiritual disease. Pride will be gone completely; irritability, covetousness, worldly mindedness, will all be gone. We shall be gentle and lovely, pure and holy – just like Jesus.

Oh the blessed prospect! Jesus will not give us up till we are altogether free from spiritual diseases. Then shall be fulfilled: 'Who heals all my diseases'.

Such is His discipline and care, that day by day there shall be done something towards this complete cure, and we should say to ourselves, 'Have I made some progress today? Am I a little freer of disease today than I was yesterday? Am I something more conformed to Jesus today?'

At the new year we should say, 'Have I made more progress during the last year than the previous one?' For the will of the Lord regarding us is that we should be like Jesus at the last; and that the will of God only needing to be presented to us, and instantaneously in our inmost souls we should be ready to do it. The Psalmist desired to be grateful to God that He was carrying on this cure (F, 1876).

Youth renewed like the eagle's

'He satisfies my desires with good things, so that my youth is renewed like the eagle's' (Ps. 103:5). Notice the figure again – the old eagles casting their feathers; and this being done, their strength renewed, and they become strong and powerful again. With those advanced in years this was the case. Thus the Psalmist looking on himself, admired what the Lord had done for him.

He does not refer to food, though that is included; and for every crumb of bread and drop of water we should be exceedingly grateful, for the body is strong and vigorous through the food given us. The Psalmist meant to say that his mouth was satisfied with good things, like that of the eagle was, through the instrumentality of good food. But more than this, he referred to spiritual food, through which his spiritual strength was renewed.

Now beloved Christian friends, this is the momentous point. There is no necessity for aged believers to get more and more lifeless and careless and worldly-minded (F, 1876).

Has God changed?

And here I bear, for the honour and glory of God, my own testimony. I am happier now, after having been a believer nearly fifty years, than I was fifty years ago; happier far than I was forty years ago, than I was thirty years ago, than

I was twenty years ago, than I was ten years ago. As the time has gone on, my peace and joy and happiness in the Lord have increased more and more, instead of going more and more.

Why do I refer to this? Not to boast, for it is all by the grace of God; but to encourage my younger fellow-believers to expect greater things from the Lord, who delights in giving abundantly. And as you sing sometimes, 'More and more, more and more', there is yet more to come.

Let us look out for it, for God delights to give more grace. It is the joy and delight of His heart to give more and more. Why should it not be? Why should we not in the last part of the life have the best things? Has God changed? Far from it! Is the Bible changed? No! We have the same blessed Word. Is the power of the Holy Spirit less? Far different from that; nothing of the kind! The Lord Jesus Christ is ever ready to bless. The Word we now have is the whole revelation. And our heavenly Father has the same heart towards His children (F, 1876).

Happiness and vigour in old age

As the Psalmist got old he did not get very worldly-minded, he did not get lifeless and cold and carnal, but his spiritual strength was renewed.

Thus it may be with us. It is a mistake to suppose that for two or three years after conversion we may be in a healthy and lively state, and after we have known the Lord for five or ten years may expect to become cold and dead and formal, and go back again little by little. Far otherwise it may be, far otherwise it ought to be; and if not, we are not living to the praise and glory of God. The Psalmist in his advanced years was more happy in the Lord, more spiritually-minded. He had more spiritual power and vigour at the end than he had at the beginning. Oh! My beloved younger brethren and sisters, you have before you not the prospects of dull and miserable days but of brighter happier days (F, 1876).

Steward or owner?

Do you consider yourself a *steward* of the means you possess, or that you are the owner thereof? The right and scriptural way is to look upon ourselves as *stewards* and not as owners of our property; for the time is approaching when stewardship will come to an end, and we shall enter into the possession of our inheritance.

The steward has to give an account of his stewardship. It is indeed by grace alone that we are saved, through faith and not by works; but this very fact should lead us the more earnestly to show our gratitude for the grace bestowed upon us, by walking consistently.

It becomes us to be *faithful* stewards. To the faithful steward the recompense is given even now in some measure while he is yet in the body; but in the world to come *the reward of grace* will be rendered according to the degree of faithfulness manifested by the steward (N4, 1880).

The conditions for successful prayer

Had it been left to us to make promises concerning prayer, I do not know that you or I could have done more than say, 'Ask and you shall receive' (Matt. 7:7–8). Yet while the promise is so full, so deep, so broad, so precious in every way, we have here – as becomes us with other parts of the Word of God – to compare Scripture with Scripture, because in other parts additions are made, or conditions given, which if we neglect will hinder our getting the full benefit of prayer.

I judge we have not to lose sight of the passage in 1 John 5:13–15 'I write these things to you who believe in the Son of God so that you may know that you have eternal life. This is the assurance we have in approaching God: that if we ask anything according to his will, he hears us. And if we know that he hears us – whatever we ask – we know that we have what we asked of him.'

Here is the first point specially to be noticed regarding prayer – 'If we ask anything according to his will he hears us. And if we know that he hears us – whatever we ask – we know we have what we asked of him.' If therefore we pray, and desire to have our petitions granted, it becomes us first to see to it that we ask for things according to His mind and will. For our blessing and happiness are intimately connected with the holiness of God (Q, 1880).

A prayer which would not be answered

Suppose there were living in Bristol a person who had long carried on a business who was known by those intimately acquainted with him to be an idle person, one who shrinks from work; or, whenever he can, gets out of it, and seeks to have an easy time of it.

Suppose such a person had heard of the promises about prayer, and should say, 'Now I will try if these things are true, and I will ask God to give me £100,000 sterling, and then I can give myself easy days; I can travel about and enjoy myself.'

163

Suppose he prays every day for this large sum of money. Will he obtain it? Assuredly not! Why not? He does not ask for it that he may help the poor; that he may contribute to the work of God more liberally, but he asks that he may spend his life in idleness, and in enjoying the pleasures of the world. He is not asking for things according to the mind of God, and therefore, however long and earnestly he may pray, he will never get the answer. We are only warranted in expecting our prayers to be answered when we ask for things which are according to the mind of God (Q, 1880).

The second condition

The second point we should notice is, that we do not ask on account of our own goodness or merit, but, as the Scripture expresses it, 'in the name of the Lord Jesus Christ'. I refer you to John 14:13–14, 'And I will do whatever you ask in my name, so that the Son may bring glory to the Father. You may ask me anything in my name and I will do it.'

The statement is given twice, in order to show the great importance of the truth; for whenever a statement is given twice in the Word of God, we may be sure a weighty and important subject is brought before us. What does this statement given twice by the Lord Jesus mean? If we desire to go to Heaven, how shall we get there? On the ground of our own goodness, merit, or worthiness? Because we are not so bad as others? Because we go regularly to a place of worship? Because we give a little to the poor?

In this way assuredly no one will get to Heaven. It is quite right to go to a place of worship. It is quite right that of the abundance God gives we should contribute to the poor. It is quite right that we should act according to morality. But in this way a poor sinner cannot get to Heaven. We must see our lost and ruined condition by nature, and that we deserve nothing but punishment. . . .

164

As by faith in the Lord Jesus Christ we shall stand before God at the last, so it is now in approaching God in prayer. If we desire to have our petitions answered, we must come to Him, not in our own name, but as sinners who trust in Jesus, who by faith in His name are united to the blessed risen Lord, who have become, through trusting in Him, members of that body of which He is the Head (Q, 1880).

Jesus is worthy

Therefore on the ground of our own goodness we cannot expect to have our prayers answered. But Jesus is worthy, and for His sake we may have our prayers answered. There is nothing too choice, too costly, or too great for God to give Him. He is worthy. He is the spotless, holy child, Who under all circumstances acted according to the mind of God. And if we trust in Him, if we hide in Him, if we put Him forward, and ourselves in the background, depend on Him and plead His name, we may expect to have our prayers answered.

Someone may say, 'I have prayed through long years for my unconverted children, but they have not yet been converted. I feel I shall not have my prayers answered. I am so unworthy.'

This is a mistake. The promises are particularly for such – for the weak, for the feeblest, for the ignorant, for the needy; for all such who ask for Christ's sake are warranted to expect their prayers to be answered.

But if it mean 'I live in sin, I go on habitually in an evil course', the prayer cannot be answered, for in Psalm 66:18 we read, 'If I had cherished sin in my heart, the Lord would not have listened.' That is, if I live in sin, and go on in a course hateful to God, I may not expect my prayers to be answered (Q, 1880).

The third condition

A third condition is that we exercise faith in the power and willingness of God to answer our prayers. This is deeply important. In Mark 11:24 we read, 'Whatever you ask in prayer, believe that you have received it, and it will be yours.'

I have found invariably in the fifty-four years and nine months during which I have been a believer, that if I only asked I was sure to get in God's time, the thing I asked for. I would especially lay this on your heart that you exercise faith in the power and willingness of God to answer your requests. We must believe that God is able and willing. To see that He is able you have only to look at the resurrection of the Lord Jesus Christ; for having raised Him from the dead, He must have almighty power. As to the love of God, you have only to look to the cross of Christ, and see His love in not sparing His Son from death. With these proofs of the power and love of God, assuredly, if we believe, we shall receive – we shall obtain (Q, 1880).

The fourth condition

Suppose now we ask, firstly, for such things as are according to the mind of God, and only such things as can be good for us; secondly, that we expect answers on the ground of the merit and righteousness of the Lord Jesus Christ, asking in His name; and thirdly that we exercise faith in the power and willingness of our Heavenly Father to grant our requests; then, fourthly, we have to continue patiently waiting on God till the blessing we seek is granted.

For observe, nothing is said in the text as to the time in which, or the circumstances under which, the prayer is to

166

be answered. 'Ask and it shall be given you.' There is a positive promise, but nothing as to the time. 'Seek and you shall find; knock and it shall be opened unto you.'

We have therefore patiently and quietly to continue waiting on God till the blessing is granted. Someone may say, 'Is it necessary I should bring a matter before God two, three, five, or even twenty times; is it not enough I tell Him once?' We might as well say there is no need to tell Him once, for He knows beforehand what our need is. He wants us to prove that we have confidence in Him, that we take our place as creatures towards the Creator (Q, 1880).

Why prayer may not be answered immediately

We are never to lose sight of the fact that there may be particular reasons why prayer may not be at once answered. One reason may be the need for the exercise of our faith, for by exercise faith is strengthened. We all know that if our faith were not exercised it would remain as it were at first. By the trial it is strengthened. Another reason may be that we may glorify God by the manifestation of patience. This is a grace by which God is greatly magnified. Our manifestation of patience glorifies God. There may be another reason. Our heart may not be prepared for the answer to our prayer.

I will give an illustration. Suppose that three weeks ago a lad of sixteen years of age had been brought to the knowledge of the Lord Jesus Christ, and that with his heart full of love to the Lord he wanted to do something for the Lord. Suppose he goes to the Sunday-school Superintendent and says, 'Will you have the kindness to give me a class to teach?'

A class of nine children is given him. Now this dear lad, whose heart is full of love to the Lord, begins to pray that

God would convert those nine children. He prays in private and before them, and also exhorts them to seek the Lord. After going home from his class, he gives himself earnestly to prayer that God would convert these nine children.

On Monday he repeats his request before God, and so day by day during the week and on Sunday again particularly; and then he goes to the class and expects that these nine children will be converted. He finds however that they are not, but that they are just in the same state as before. He again sets the Gospel before them; he exhorts, beseeches, and weeps before them. During the second week his prayers are most earnest, but on the following Sunday he finds that none of the nine children are yet converted.

Does it mean that God will not answer these prayers? It cannot be that this dear lad will have to go on praying, and God not regard it. But the reason is that the heart of this lad is not prepared for the blessing. If these children had been converted the first week, he would take credit to himself; he would think what he had been able to do, and would attribute the conversions to his entreaties, instead of to the power of the Holy Spirit. He would take credit to himself, though he might not be aware of it. But let him go patiently on, and when his heart is prepared for the blessing, God will give it (Q, 1880).

Everyday answers to prayer

All the children of God, who walk in His ways and wait on Him in prayer, have, more or less frequently, answers to prayer. I will illustrate this. All who in any measure walk before God at the close of the day thank Him for His mercies, and commend themselves to Him for protection during the night. In the morning they find that no fire has happened and no wicked hands have molested them. Here

168

is an answer to prayer and we have to thank God for it. The more we observe these matters, the more we find how we get prayer answered.

Many that have suffered from sleeplessness have often, in answer to prayer, had sound refreshing sleep, and have had in the morning to thank God for it.

Now all, on the other hand, have sometimes long to wait for answers to prayer. Many of the dear children of God have long to wait for the conversion of their children. While some receive the blessing very soon, others have to wait for many years. I have had immediate answers to prayer, so many that I could reckon them by tens of thousands.

If I say that during the fifty-four years and nine months that I have been a believer I have had thirty thousand answers to prayer either in the same hour or the same day that the requests were made I should not go a particle too far. Often before leaving the bedroom in the morning have I had prayer answered that was offered that morning, and in the course of the day I have had five or six more answers to prayer; so that at least thirty thousand prayers have been answered the same day or hour that they were offered (Q, 1880).

Answers which take longer

But you may suppose all my prayers have been thus promptly answered. No, not all of them. Sometimes I have had to wait for weeks, months or years; sometimes many years. The man speaking at the present time, whom God has delighted to honour by giving thirty thousand answers to prayer in the same hour or day on which they were offered, this same man has had to wait many years for answers to many of his prayers.

During the first six weeks of the year 1866 I heard of the

conversion of six persons for whom I had been praying for a long time. For one I had been praying between two and three years; for another between three and four years; for another above seven years; for the fourth above ten years; for the fifth above fifteen years; and for the sixth above twenty years.

I once asked a thing of God, which I knew to be according to His mind, and though I brought it day by day and generally many times a day before Him, in such assurance as to be able to thank Him hundreds of times for the answer before it was received, yet I had to wait three years and ten months before the blessing was given to me. At another time I had to wait six years; at another time eleven and a half years. In the last case I brought the matter about twenty thousand times before God, and invariably in the fullest assurance of faith, and yet eleven and a half years passed before the answer was given (Q, 1880).

Still waiting after thirty-six years

In one instance my faith has been tried even more than this. In November 1844, I began to pray for the conversion of five individuals. I prayed every day without one single interruption, whether sick or in health, on the land or on the sea, and whatever the pressure of my engagements might be. Eighteen months elapsed before the first of the five was converted. I thanked God, and prayed on for the others. Five years elapsed, and then the second was converted. I thanked God for the second, and prayed on for the other three. Day by day I continued to pray for them, and six more years passed before the third was converted. I thanked God for the three, and went on praying for the other two. These two remain unconverted.

The man to whom God in the riches of His grace has

170

given tens of thousands of answers to prayer, in the same hour or day in which they were offered, has been praying day by day for nearly thirty-six years for the conversion of these two individuals, and yet they remain unconverted; for next November it will be thirty-six years since I began to pray for their conversion. But I hope in God, I pray on, and look for the answer (Q, 1880).

One of the two men, for whom Müller had prayed for thirty-six years was converted before Müller died and the other became a Christian after Müller's death.

Praying together

There is one point I would especially lay on the hearts of my beloved brethren and sisters, and that is – united prayer. In Matthew 18:19, the Lord Jesus says – 'If two of you on earth agree about anything you ask for, it will be done for you by my Father in Heaven.' If therefore there are brethren and sisters in Christ who have unconverted relatives, and if they could unite with two or more persons, and unitedly ask God to convert their children, oh, what blessing might not come in this way? They would plead this promise before the Lord, read it out when they meet, and put their finger – so to speak – upon it.

If they meet once a week for half an hour, or once a fortnight, or as often as they conveniently could, to plead this promise before the Lord, after a while a father would have to say, 'My son, who almost broke my heart, has been converted', and a mother, 'I have a letter from my daughter, who fifteen years ago left my home, and has been living in sin, telling me she has found the Lord Jesus Christ.'

How their faith would be strengthened by such united prayer and testimonies! After a while, as their faith was strengthened, they would unitedly pray for their pastor,

that God would bless his labours in the conversion of
sinners, and in blessing upon the Church; and as they got
further enlarged their prayer would extend to missions, the
circulation of the Scriptures and tracts. They would know
the power and blessedness of prayer more and more
abundantly, and would wait earnestly upon God, asking
Him yet once more, in these days, to grant a mighty revival
in the Church of Christ at large (Q, 1880).

Keep a record of your answers

I have found it a great blessing to treasure up in the memory
the answers God graciously gives me. I have always kept a
record to strengthen the memory. I advise the keeping of a
little memorandum book. On one side – say the left hand
side – put down the petition and the date when you began to
offer it. Let the opposite page be blank to put down the
answer in each case, and you will soon find how many
answers you get, and thus you will be encouraged more and
more, your faith will be strengthened; and especially you
will see what a lovely, bountiful and gracious Being God is.
Your heart will go out more and more in love to God, and
you will say, 'It is my Heavenly Father who has been so
kind, I will trust in Him, I will confide in Him' (Q, 1880).

The personal return of Jesus . . .

In the days of the apostles, the disciples were comforted
and encouraged by the prospect of the personal return
of the Lord Jesus Christ. An angel had said to them as

they watched the Lord depart from earth, 'Men of Galilee, why do you stand here looking into the sky? This same Jesus, who has been taken from you into Heaven, will come back in the same way you have seen him go into Heaven' (Acts 1:11).

This, and not death, was the hope of the Church; and thus it ought to have remained up to His actual return. His coming should have continued to be the hope of the Church; but this alas! for centuries has not been the case.

In confessions of faith the truth that the Lord Jesus will come again may still have a place; but practically to by far the greater number of His disciples it has been a *mere doctrinal statement* that has not been enjoyed, and which has had no influence upon their lives. The Lord, however, desired it should be otherwise. He intended that His Church should look for Him; that she should watch and wait for His return. Again and again, during His personal ministry, the Lord Jesus foretold this great event; and after His ascension the apostles referred continually to it (T, 1881).

. . . proved in Scripture

Very many passages of Scripture might be quoted in proof of this assertion, but I will mention only the following:

'When the Son of Man *comes in his glory*, and all the angels with him, he will sit on his throne in heavenly glory' (Matt. 25:31).

'In my Father's house are many rooms; if it were not so, I would have told you. And if I go and prepare a place for you, I will *come back* and take you to be with me that you also may be where I am' (John 14:2–3).

'Just as man is destined to die once, and after that to face judgment, so Christ was sacrificed once to take away the

173

sins of many people; and he will *appear a second time*, no
to bear sin, but to bring salvation to those who are waiting
for him' (Heb. 9:27–8).

'For the Lord Himself will *come down from Heaven* with
a loud command, with the voice of the archangel and with
the trumpet call of God, and the dead in Christ will rise
first. After that, we who are still alive and are left will be
caught up with them in the clouds to meet the Lord in the
air. And so will we be with the Lord for ever' (1 Thess
4:16–17).

These quotations will suffice to prove that the second
coming of the Lord Jesus means that He will return *in
person*, and has no reference to the gift of the Holy Spirit on
the day of Pentecost, nor to His manifesting Himself in an
especial manner to the believer in the way of comfort,
instruction, or help of any kind; nor has it reference to our
death, when we, as believers, are taken up to be with Him
(T, 1881).

. . . why stress it?

If anyone should say, 'Why lay such stress upon this; is not
our going to Him when we die the same thing?' The reply is,
'There is a vast difference between these two events.'

(a) As *individuals* we shall at that time be brought only to
a state of *partial* happiness; we shall have no glorified
bodies *then*, but must await the hour when 'in a flash, in
the twinkling of an eye, at the last trumpet . . . the dead will
be raised imperishable, and we will be changed' (1 Cor.
15:52). Nor when we fall asleep do we reign with Christ and
sit with Him upon the throne; because He will not then be
manifestly reigning. Blessed therefore though it is for the
child of God, when he departs, 'to be absent from the body
and present with the Lord', it will be unspeakably *more*

blessed still to enter upon that *fulness* of glory which awaits us only at our Lord's return.

(b) Satan will not be bound until Jesus comes again; and for this reason, by the permission of God, he still has power here, both in the world and in the Church, though individuals are out of his reach who have fallen asleep in Jesus.

(c) *The whole Church* will at once be introduced to full eternal happiness and glory at our blessed Lord's return. Not only as *individuals* will our cup of joy be full to overflowing, but we shall rejoice throughout eternity with *the whole company of the redeemed.*

What has been said therefore is, I trust, sufficient to show that the second coming of Christ will be His *personal* return, and that there is a vast difference between the death of individual believers and the coming advent of our Lord in glory (T, 1881).

. . . some accompanying events

I now proceed to consider briefly *some* of the events which will take place *then*.

The first resurrection, when the changed and risen saints together will be caught up to meet the Lord in the air, to be forever with Him (1 Thess. 4:16–17). At this time those only will be raised who, as believers in the Messiah under the old covenant dispensation, or as disciples of the Lord Jesus under that of the new covenant, shall have fallen asleep in Him. The commonly received opinion is that at our Lord's return there will be a *general* resurrection, both of believers and unbelievers, while the Holy Spirit teaches in the Holy Scriptures that they who are *Christ's* and they only, will have part in the first resurrection . . . [A passage follows in which Müller discusses 1 Corinthians

175

15:22–3; 1 Thessalonians 4:16–17; Revelation 20:4–6, 11–15; Revelation 6:9.]

The conversion and restoration of Israel nationally (who will have returned to their own land in *unbelief*); for in Scripture the glory and resurrection of the Church of the first-born ones is always connected with the time when Israel again 'shall know the Lord' (Ps. 102:16). See Jeremiah 30 and 31; Isaiah 11 and 12. Read also carefully Isaiah 24, 25, 26, and 27 (T, 1881).

. . . two more events

Another event which will take place at the return of the Lord Jesus is that *Satan will be bound* (Rev. 20:1–3). During the present dispensation, *before* the return of our Lord, Satan will not be bound; therefore sin and open wickedness will continue to the end of it; and instead of becoming better, things, according to Scripture, will *become worse and worse* . . . But this state of things will not always last; for, when Jesus comes again, Satan will *lose* his power in the earth, and will be shut up in the bottomless pit for a thousand years.

Another event will be *the separation between the wheat and the tares*, who represent Christendom, or the professing church of Christ. Read carefully Matthew 13:24–30; also verses 37–43. In this parable, together with our Lord's own explanation of it, we see what is to be expected during this present dispensation. Civilisation, mental cultivation, and advancement in knowledge of every kind may continue to the utmost; but man, fallen man, remains *a ruined creature*, except he be regenerated by the power of the Holy Spirit, through the acceptance of the Gospel.

Intellectually he may be improved and polished to the very highest degree, but he is a *sinner*, and, in his natural

176

condition, remains lost, ruined and undone. He may even possess natural religion and a form of godliness; but if he is not born again he is still at enmity with God, and as assuredly as he does not believe in the Lord Jesus Christ 'God's wrath remains on him' (John 3:36), (T, 1881).

. . . compared with a common notion

The notion entertained by many godly, excellent persons, that the world will be *converted during the present dispensation* by the preaching of the Gospel, and that the millennium will thus finally be introduced is not according to the Holy Scriptures.

The Gospel, indeed, was to be preached 'as a *testimony* to all nations'. but it was not to be the means of the *conversion* of the world (Matt. 24:14). Moreover, from Acts 15:14 we learn the character of the present dispensation, which is, that God *takes out* from among the Gentiles a people for His name, but does not *convert* all nations. This is confirmed by the parable of the wheat and the tares; for if the whole world were to be converted before the return of the Lord Jesus, there would be no truth in the explanation given of it by our Lord Himself. He tells us that the tares (the children of the wicked one) were to grow together with the wheat (the children of the kingdom) until the end of the age, namely, up to the time of His own return.

This, therefore, the Word of the Lord Jesus, is in direct opposition to the common notion that the world will be converted previous to His coming again (T, 1881).

. . . preceded by certain events

From 2 Thessalonians 2:1–8 we learn that the Lord Jesus will not come until after the manifestation of 'the apostasy'. Has the apostasy here spoken of taken place, and has the man of lawlessness (or, the Antichrist) been revealed? The reply from Scripture is, the apostasy has *not* yet taken place, and the man of lawlessness has *not* yet been revealed.

This passage has not found its fulfilment either in popery or the popes. Fearful as the delusions of popery are, and awful as is the picture of what the popes have been, the apostasy here referred to will be far *more dreadful still*; for it will be no less than an entire renunciation of all that is divine, and the setting up as God of the man of lawlessness himself. For he 'even sets himself up in God's temple, proclaiming himself to be God' (v. 4).

He will be a king, a mighty monarch, whose might is obtained through the energy given to him by Satan, for 'the dragon gave the beast his power and his throne and great authority' (Rev. 13:2). This king, the Antichrist, will be at the head of the *ten kingdoms* of the Roman earth (that is, the ten kingdoms into which the countries which formerly constituted the Roman Empire will be finally divided), and the ten kings will agree to give to him their power.

During the period of his especial glory, which will be only forty-two months, he will blaspheme God, His tabernacle, and those that dwell in Heaven. It will also be given to him to make war with the saints and to overcome them; and he will be given authority over every tribe, people, language and nation. And all inhabitants of the earth shall worship him, 'all whose names have not been written in the book of life belonging to the Lamb that was slain from the creation of the world' (Rev. 13:5–8), (T, 1881).

. . . longing for His return

This, then, and not the world's conversion, is the state of things towards which we are rapidly hastening. Do we all really *believe* what the Scriptures declare concerning the things that are coming upon the earth, that the time is speeding on when 'no-one could buy or sell unless he had the mark, which is the name of the beast or the number of his name' (Rev. 13:17): when *whoever* will not submit to *this* and worship him, must be prepared to lose his life?

The *end*, however, of this lawless one is plainly foretold in Scripture: whom the Lord Jesus will 'overthrow with the breath of his mouth and destroy by the splendour of his coming' (2 Thess. 2:8).

We have now in the next place to consider that it is the will of the Lord that we, His disciples, should wait for His return. A great many passages might be quoted from the New Testament in proof of this; but, for the sake of brevity, I will refer only to a few . . . [He discusses Titus 2:11–13; Matthew 24:36–41; 25:13; Mark 13:35–7; Revelation 16:15.]

Now, are we as believers, all *watching*? Are we earnestly *longing* for the return of that blessed One? Do our hearts truly yearn after Him, and long for His glorious appearing? Are we also doing our part to hasten on His coming? And is it habitually our *prayer* that the Lord will be pleased to hasten the fulfilment of the events yet to be fulfilled before that day comes? (T, 1881).

. . . and some deeply important questions

Finally we must consider the *practical* effect this truth should have upon our hearts. If it be really received and entered into, the child of God will say, 'What can I do for my blessed Saviour before He comes again? How can I most glorify Him? His will concerning me is that I should occupy "until He come". How then can I best use for Him the talents with which I am entrusted, my physical strength, my mental powers? How can my sight, my tongue, all my faculties of mind and body be best devoted to His praise? How should my time, my money, all that I am and have be used for Him? How can my whole spirit, soul, and body be best consecrated to His service?'

These are deeply important practical questions which all believers in the Lord Jesus should ask themselves, seeing that we are not our own, but are bought with a price, even with His precious blood.

Instead of indulging in inactivity and listlessness on account of the evil state of things around us, we should pray and work, and work and pray, as if it were in *our* power to stem the torrent of abounding iniquity; for who can say *how much good* one single child of God who is thoroughly in earnest may accomplish; and how greatly he may glorify God by walking in entire separation from all that is hateful to Him?

We have especially also to guard against the temptation of slackening our efforts for the conversion of sinners, because the world will not be converted before Jesus comes. Rather should we say, 'The time of His coming may be soon; what therefore can I do to warn sinners, and to win souls for Him?' (T, 1881).

A deadly spiritual disease

Sin is not, as some suppose, a *comparatively little thing*. It is a deadly spiritual disease, as the Word of God declares it to be; and no progress in education, no mental culture, can eradicate it from the heart, nor change depraved human nature. For, notwithstanding every effort at improvement, the heart *remains* 'deceitful above all things and beyond cure' (Jer. 17:9).

Until the return of the Lord Jesus, therefore, the present state of things, will *continue*, and will become worse and worse . . . . (T, 1881).

I am indeed a hell-deserving sinner. By nature I am a lost man, but I am a sinner saved by the grace of God. Though I am by nature a sinner, I do not live in sin; I hate sin; I hate it more and more; and I love holiness; yes, I love holiness more and more (W, 1897).

In Poland: sceptics melted to tears

After our departure from St Petersburg, we left for Warsaw, the capital of Russian Poland, where I held six meetings only, and then we went to the neighbourhood of Pruszkow. Here I preached once, at an orphan institution, and from there we proceeded to Lodz, the second largest city in Russian Poland, which is full of factories.

My service began on a Wednesday evening at half past eight; but though this hour seemed unfavourable, I found the chapel at which I preached crowded to the utmost, and about 150 persons had to stand during the whole of the service. Altogether there were about 1,200 persons present. On Thursday and Friday evening it was the same. On Sunday, twice the place was crowded as before, and so it was on Monday evening.

By this time I heard from the pastor, from a Christian colporteur, and from others, that almost the whole town seemed moved by my preaching, and that it was the topic of conversation at many of the factories of the city, at the public houses, and in families generally.

I was told also that on the previous evening a number of

'freethinkers' as they are called, that is sceptics or infidels, had been at the meeting, who left, melted to tears. The next morning I received a note in German, of which the following is a translation. 'I, and almost the whole population of this town, in the name of the Lord Jesus, entreat that you will have the kindness to remain with us until after next Sunday. In the name of many thousands, I thank you for your ministry.' The crowds who came at first continued to attend *all* the meetings, and at the twelfth service, the number of persons present, was as large as it was at the beginning; that is to say there were about 1,200, as many as could possibly be accommodated. There is good reason to believe that the Spirit of God worked mightily amongst them (N4, 1883).

The grandeur of God's world

In India –

From Calcutta we went to Darjeeling, on the Himalayas, about 8,000 feet above the level of the sea, where I preached five times during our stay of six days, and conversed a good deal with various Christians. The cold was severe, and was felt by us all the more after experiencing the heat of the Red Sea, and of Madras.

On the fifth day of our stay at Darjeeling the sky was clear enough for us to see the highest mountain range in the world, which is perpetually covered with snow. Kinchinjunga (the second highest mountain on the globe, twenty-eight thousand feet above the level of the sea) though 45 miles distant, could be clearly seen; but Mount Everest, the highest mountain in the world, twenty-nine thousand feet high, was not visible, as it cannot be seen without going to a spot six miles from Darjeeling. The amazing grandeur and magnificence of this mountain range will never be erased from the mind of any God-fearing person who has seen it (N4, 1884).

In Switzerland –

After our departure from Hauptweil on the morning of December 26, we travelled to Chur, a town situated in a very picturesque and mountainous district on the east of Switzerland. In the course of our railway journey to that place, whilst the weather was bitterly cold, we observed the high mountains in every direction covered with snow, noticed large masses of thick ice floating on the rivers and lakes, and found the frost most severe during the whole of our visit to that beautiful locality (A, 1890).

Systematic giving

Are you giving *systematically* to the Lord's work, or are you leaving it to feeling, to impression made upon you through particular circumstances, or to striking appeals? If we do not give from principle *systematically*, we shall find that our one brief life is gone before we are aware of it, and that, in return, we have done little for that adorable One who bought us with His precious blood, and to whom belongs all we have and are.

As the Lord is pleased to entrust us with means by the labour of our hands, or in our business or profession, or even through presents, legacies, or in any other way we may be supplied by Him with means, we should consider that we are His stewards, and that He would have us to use our money for Him. By this I do not mean that ordinarily we should give away all that we possess as fast as we receive anything from the Lord; but, after considering our duty to our families and other particular obligations, we should ask ourselves, 'How much can I now spare for the poor or the work of God?'

As the Lord *prospers* us, as *He entrusts us with means*, we should give, or lay aside for giving till calls are made upon us. The *principle* of thus acting is plainly set forth in 1 Corinthians 16:2 'On the first day of every week, each one of you should set aside a sum of money in keeping with his income.' This passage, it is well known, refers as to its literal application to a collection to be made for the poor Jewish believers in Palestine who were in need at the time this letter was written to the Church at Corinth; but, though this is the case, the *principle* laid down in it holds good *now* (N4, 1885).

On the way to the Father's house

We are to love those who do not care in the least for us. We are to love those who do not walk with us on the road to Heaven, and whom we have never seen or heard of; that is the will of our heavenly Father regarding us.

We ought to look lovingly on weak disciples, and you and I, instead of looking at their weakness and shortcomings, ought to seek to find out Christ in them. If we do so, we shall find how dear they will become to our hearts, and we shall love them.

How deeply important to keep this before us in the divine life, that we manifest the mind of Christ. Just as that Blessed One sought not to please Himself, but to be the servant of others, so have we to imitate that Blessed One.

Though not yet perfect in love, we are to aim after that for which we have been apprehended of God in Christ Jesus. We ought to love one another in spite of the weaknesses and infirmities we see in one another.

We are left here to be representatives of the Lord Jesus Christ in this world. This great honour He has bestowed upon us here.

God is love, and he who loves most is most like God. All the members of the heavenly family should remember the precious blood that bought them, and love one another whilst on the way to their Father's house (W, undated).

Holding on to truth

In India –

On January 2, 1890, we left Allahabad for Jubbulpore. During our stay in this city I preached fourteen times in various churches, with great help from the Lord. While thus quietly and happily going on in my service at Jubbulpore, a letter was handed to me from a missionary at Agra, to whom Mr Wright had sent a telegram, that he might inform me of the death of my beloved daughter, his wife.

Our plans were now completely altered, and it was obvious, after prayer, that we ought as soon as possible to return to England, and see what could be done to fill up the place of my dear daughter, who for nearly thirty years had gratuitously laboured at the orphan houses, but who had died in Bristol in the 58th year of her age. We decided therefore that by the first suitable steamer from Bombay we would return to England.

I pause here for a moment. Mrs Wright was my only child, who for nearly forty-four years had sought to walk in the ways of God. Without any previous information of her illness, this announcement came suddenly to me. To many persons this would have been a heavy blow, and so it was to me. For I greatly loved my daughter. But my heart remained in perfect peace, because I took this affliction as

I had taken former heavy trials – out of the hand of my heavenly Father. I fully realised that He had taken her to Himself, and had done therefore to her the very best thing that could happen, and that to me this event would work for my good.

Because then, as I believed Romans 8:28 to contain the truth of God, and was assured that it would be even so in my own experience, my heart remained in peace, perfect peace. May all my beloved fellow-believers seek to lay hold on the truth contained in Romans 8:28, if they have not as yet done so, in order that, under heavy trials, their hearts may be in peace (A, 1890).

How to discover God's will

I seek at the beginning to get my heart into such a state that it has no will of its own in a given matter. Nine-tenths of the trouble with people generally is just here. Nine-tenths of the difficulties are overcome when our hearts are ready to do the Lord's will, whatever it may be. When one truly is in this state, it is usually but a little way to the knowledge of what His will is.

Having done this, I do not leave the result to feeling or simple impression. If so, I make myself liable to great delusions.

I seek the will of the Spirit of God through, or in connection with, the Word of God. The Spirit and the Word must be combined. If I look to the Spirit alone without the Word, I lay myself open to great delusions also. If the Holy Spirit guides us at all, He will do it according to the Scriptures and never contrary to them.

Next I take into account providential circumstances. These often plainly indicate God's will in connection with His Word and Spirit.

I ask God in prayer to reveal His will to me aright.

Thus, through prayer to God, the study of the Word and reflection, I come to a deliberate judgment according to the best of my ability and knowledge; and if my mind is thus at peace, and continues so after two or three petitions, I proceed accordingly. In trivial matters, and in transactions involving more important issues, I have found this method always effective (G, 1895).

The refreshing friend

'He restores my soul' (Ps. 23:3). It is the very joy and delight of the heart of our precious Lord Jesus Christ to refresh us spiritually. If at any time we are cast down, through trials and difficulties, or through sore temptations, which we have to encounter, and we find that we are not being refreshed, what we should do is to remind the Lord Jesus Christ that He has been given 'an instructed tongue, to know the word that sustains the weary' (Isa. 50:4). I advise all my beloved brethren and sisters in Christ to make more use than they have yet done of this blessed word in Isaiah.

O let us, in childlike simplicity, trust our precious, precious Lord Jesus Christ! Whenever you are cast down, whenever you are greatly tried spiritually, open your heart to the precious Jesus, as your friend. I have done it for many a long year, and it is just this which upholds me, which comforts me, which makes me a happy man.

I deal with my precious Lord Jesus as a bosom friend. I pour out my whole heart to Him, and tell Him everything. I beg and entreat Him, whenever I need it, to speak to me a word in season, that the weariness may pass away, and that I may be refreshed spiritually. And I find Him ever ready to help me (R, 1897)

'So happy, I can scarcely bear it'

'You anoint my head with oil; my cup overflows' (Ps. 23:5). In the East, when a great one invited anyone of his friends to take a meal with him, to spend a day with him, one of the first things was not only that the servants should hand him water to wash his feet, but oil to anoint his head. As a mark of respect and reverence this was done. That was the welcome, so to speak, given to the guest who came to the house of the great one.

Now, we have no such thing done to us, but something infinitely more precious. The Holy Spirit is given to us – the Holy Spirit again and again represented under the figure of oil. And as assuredly as we have the Holy Spirit given to us, so surely shall we get to Heaven, so surely shall we share the glory of Christ, so surely shall we become like Christ and have our glorified bodies. These are the things which are implied in the gift of the Holy Spirit! How precious these things are!

If the heart were habitually given to these things, it would be full of joy! We should be exceedingly happy; and therefore my affectionate counsel and advice to my beloved fellow-believers is seek more and more to ponder all this, with application to your own hearts, in order that your joy may increase more abundantly. And what will come of it at last? You will be able to say with the Psalmist, 'My cup overflows' – 'I am so happy a man that I can scarcely bear it; I not only have something in my cup, and a good deal in my cup, and have my cup full, but my cup overflows' (R, 1897).

Moving the hearts of men

Early in the summer of 1897, less than a year before Müller died, Charles Parsons visited him in his study in No. 3 Orphan House on Ashley Down. Parsons asked, 'You have

188

always found the Lord faithful to His promise?' Müller replied –

Always, for nearly seventy years every need in connection with this work has been supplied. The orphans, from the first until now, have numbered 9,500, but they have never wanted a meal. Never! Hundreds of times we have commenced the day without a penny in hand, but our heavenly Father has sent supplies by the moment they were actually required. There never was a time when we had no wholesome meal.

During all these years I have been enabled to trust in God, in the living God, and in Him alone. One million four hundred thousand pounds have been sent to me in answer to prayer. We have needed as much as £50,000 in one year, and it has all come by the time it has been really needed. No man on earth can say that I have ever asked him for a penny. We have no committees, no collectors, no voting, and no endowments. All has come in answer to believing prayer.

My trust has been in God alone; He has many ways of moving the hearts of men to help us all over the world. While I am praying He speaks to this one and another, on this continent and on that to send us help (V, 1897).

Saving for yourself

During the course of his conversation with Müller, Parsons asked him whether he had ever thought of saving money for himself. Parsons recorded – 'I shall not soon forget the dignified manner with which I was answered by this mighty man of faith. Hitherto, he had been sitting opposite me, with his knees almost close to mine, with clasped hands, and eyes that betokened a calm, quiet, and meditative spirit. Most of

*the time he leaned forward with his gaze directed towards the
floor. But now, he sat erect, and looked for several moments
into my face with an earnestness that seemed to penetrate
through my very soul. There was a grandeur and majesty
about those undimmed eyes, so accustomed to spiritual
visions, and to looking into the deep things of God.*

*'I do not know whether the question seemed to him a
sordid one, or whether it touched, shall I say, a lingering
remnant of the old self to which he so often alludes in all his
discourses. Anyhow, there was no shadow of doubt that it
aroused his whole being. After a brief pause, during which
his face was a sermon, and the depths of his clear eyes flashed
fire, he unbuttoned his coat and drew from his pocket an
old-fashioned purse, with rings in the middle separating the
character of the coins. He placed it in my hand, saying –'*

All I am possessed of is in that purse – every penny! Save
for myself! Never! When money is sent to me for my own
use I pass it on to God. As much as one thousand pounds
has thus been sent at one time, but I do not regard these
gifts as belonging to me; they belong to Him, Whose I am,
and Whom I serve. Save for myself! I dare not save; it
would be dishonouring to my loving, gracious, all-bountiful
Father (V, 1897).

Advice from an old man

*Parsons ended his interview by asking Müller to give him
some advice on his own work for God. Müller replied –*

Seek entirely to depend on God for everything. Put
yourself and your work into His hands. When thinking of
any new undertaking, ask, 'Is this agreeable to the mind of
God? Is it for His glory?' If it is not for His glory, it is not for

your good, and you must have nothing to do with it. Mind that!

Having settled that a certain course is for the glory of God, begin it in His name, and continue it to the end. Undertake it in prayer and faith, and never give up! Pray, pray, pray. Do not regard iniquity in your heart; if you do, the Lord will not hear you. Keep that before you always. Then trust in God. Depend only on God. Wait on Him. Believe on Him. Expect great things from Him. Faint not if the blessing tarries. Pray, pray, pray! And above all, rely only and alone upon the merits of our ever adorable Lord and Saviour, that according to His infinite merits, and not your own, the prayers you offer, and the work you do, will be accepted (V, 1897).

The precious prospect

Four days before he died, Müller concluded an address at Alma Road Chapel, Clifton, with these words, spoken shortly before the Lord's supper was celebrated –

O how pitifully, how mercifully, how tenderly, how graciously the Lord has been dealing with us in Christ Jesus! And what He has been doing and is doing, He will continue to do to the end of our earthly pilgrimage – He will not leave us nor forsake us, and a little while, and then He takes us home to Himself. O the bright, glorious prospect which we poor, miserable sinners have through faith in Christ Jesus!

And at last taken home to be for ever with the Lord, and to see that lovely One who laid down His life for us, ourselves being permitted to kiss His feet, ourselves being permitted to kiss His hands! O the precious prospect that awaits us! . . .

How our hearts should go forth continually in the deepest and liveliest gratitude to the Lord Jesus Christ for laying down His life for us, for shedding His blood for the remission of our sins! And how full of gratitude our hearts should be that . . . we have been made as clean, as spotless as if we had never in our whole life been guilty of one sinful action: as if we had never uttered one single unholy word, and as if there had never been found in us a thought contrary to the mind of God.

This is the position into which we are brought through faith in the Lord Jesus Christ, so that during the remainder of our life, and throughout eternity, never one single sin shall be brought against us. O the precious blood of Christ! (A, 1898).